The New Economics

The New Economics

A Manifesto

Steve Keen

polity

First published in 2022 by Polity Press

Polity Press
65 Bridge Street
Cambridge CB2 1UR, UK

Polity Press
101 Station Landing
Suite 300
Medford, MA 02155, USA

ISBN-13: 978-1-5095-4528-5
ISBN-13: 978-1-5095-4529-2 (pb)

A catalogue record for this book is available from the British Library.

Typeset in 11 on 13 pt Sabon
by Fakenham Prepress Solutions, Fakenham, Norfolk NR21 8NL
Printed and bound in Great Britain by TJ Books Ltd, Padstow, Cornwall

The publisher has used its best endeavours to ensure that the URLs for external websites referred to in this book are correct and active at the time of going to press. However, the publisher has no responsibility for the websites and can make no guarantee that a site will remain live or that the content is or will remain appropriate.

Every effort has been made to trace all copyright holders, but if any have been overlooked the publisher will be pleased to include any necessary credits in any subsequent reprint or edition.

For further information on Polity, visit our website: politybooks.com

Contents

Figures and tables

Figures

Tables

Dedicated to my wife Nisa, whose Buddhist grounding in the present keeps me sane as I contemplate the future facing both humanity, and the biosphere that humanity has so severely damaged.

1
Why this manifesto?

Even before the Covid-19 crisis began, the global economy was not in good shape, and neither was economic theory. The biggest economic crisis since the Great Depression began late in the first decade of the twenty-first century. Called the 'Global Financial Crisis' (GFC) in most of the world, and the 'Great Recession' in the United States, it saw unemployment explode from 4.6 per cent of the US workforce in early 2007 to 10 per cent in late 2009. The S&P500 stock market index, which had boomed from under 800 points in 2002 to over 1,500 in mid-2007, crashed to under 750 by early 2009. Inflation of 5.6 per cent in mid-2008 turned into deflation of 2 per cent in mid-2009.

The US economy recovered very slowly, under the influence of an unprecedented range of government interventions, from the 'Cash for Clunkers' scheme that encouraged consumers to dump old cars and buy new ones, to 'Quantitative Easing', where the Federal Reserve purchased a trillion-dollars-worth of bonds from the financial sector every year, in an attempt to stimulate the economy by making the wealthy wealthier.

The crisis, and the sluggish recovery from it, surprised both the economists who advise governments on economic policy, and the academics who develop the theories and write the textbooks that train new economists. Not only had they expected a continuation of the boom conditions that had preceded the crisis, *they in fact believed that crises could not occur.*

In his Presidential Address to the American Economic Association in January 2003, Nobel Prize winner Robert Lucas declared that crises like the Great Depression could never occur again, because 'Macroeconomics ... has succeeded: *Its central problem of depression prevention has been solved, for all practical purposes, and has in fact been solved for many decades*' (Lucas 2003, p. 1). Just two months before the crisis began, the Chief Economist of the Organization for Economic Cooperation and Development (OECD), the world's premier economic policy body, declared that '*the current economic situation is in many ways better than what we have experienced in years*', and predicted that in 2008, 'sustained growth in OECD economies would be under-pinned by strong job creation and falling unemployment' (Cotis 2007, p. 7, emphasis added). In the depths of the crisis, George W. Bush's Chief Economic Advisor Edward Lazear argued that, because the downturn had been so deep, the recovery would be very strong (Lazear and Marron 2009, Chart 1-9, p. 54). He was bitterly disappointed by the actual outcome, which was the slowest recovery from an economic crisis since the Great Depression itself.

How could economists be so wrong about the economy?

They could be excused their failure to see the Great Recession coming if the crisis were something like Covid-19, when a new pathogen suddenly emerged out of China. As long ago as 1995, Laurie Garrett declared that such a plague was inevitable (Garrett 1995). But predicting *when* the pathogen would emerge, let alone what its characteristics would be, was clearly impossible. However, the epicentre of the Great Recession was the US financial system itself: the crisis came from *inside* the economy, rather than from outside. Surely there were warning signs? As Queen Elizabeth herself put it when she attended a briefing at the London School of Economics in 2008, 'If these things were so large, how come everyone missed them?' (Greenhill 2008).

Not all economists did: there were some who warned that a crisis was not merely likely, but imminent. The Dutch economist Dirk Bezemer identified a dozen, of whom I was one (Bezemer 2009a, 2009b, 2010; Keen 1995, 2007). Though these economists came from disparate backgrounds, Bezemer noted that they had one *negative* characteristic in common: 'no one predicted the crisis on the basis of a neo-classical framework' (Bezemer 2010, p. 678).

One would expect that the failure by economists to anticipate the biggest economic event of the post-Second World War world would cause economics to change dramatically. But it hasn't. What Bezemer called 'Neoclassical economics' was the dominant approach to modelling the economy before the GFC, and it has remained dominant since.[1]

The failure of economics to reform itself after such a profound empirical failure has led to strong criticism of economics from within – even by economists who have been awarded the Nobel Prize in Economics. Robert Solow, the 1987 recipient, told a United States Congressional Hearing into economics in 2010 that:

> We are in desperate need of jobs, and the approach to macroeconomics that dominates the elite universities of the country and many central banks and other influential policy circles, that approach seems to have essentially nothing to say about the problem. (Solow 2010, p. 12)

Paul Romer, who received the Prize in 2018, argued in 2016 that economics had such a 'noncommittal relationship with the truth' that it deserved the label of 'post-real' (Romer 2016, p. 5).

These criticisms of Neoclassical economics by prominent Neoclassical economists echo criticisms that economists from other schools of thought have been making for many decades. These rival approaches to economics are very different to the specializations that exist in sciences like physics. Some physicists specialize in General Relativity, others in Quantum Mechanics, Statistical Mechanics, Newtonian physics, and so on. Each of these approaches has different perspectives on how the Universe operates, but each works very well in its respective domain: General Relativity in the realm of the very large (the Universe), Quantum Mechanics in the realm of the very small (the atom), while Newton's equations work very well in between, and so on.

But in economics, different schools of thought have visions of how the economy works that are fundamentally in conflict. There is no way to partition the economy into sections where Neoclassical economics applies and others where rival schools of thought like Post Keynesian, Austrian or Biophysical economics apply. On the same topic – say, for example, the role of private debt in causing financial crises – these schools of thought will often have answers that flatly contradict Neoclassical economics, and frequently also, each other. These non-mainstream schools of thought, which are collectively known as 'heterodox' economics, are followed by a significant minority of academic economists – as many as 10 per cent of the discipline, going on a campaign in France in 2015 to establish a separate classification there (Lavoie 2015b; Orléan 2015).[2]

The economists who did warn of the Global Financial Crisis came almost exclusively from these dissenting schools of thought.[3] Though they differed from each other in significant ways, Bezemer noted that they shared 'a concern with financial assets as distinct from real-sector assets, with the credit flows that finance both forms of wealth, with the debt growth accompanying growth in financial wealth, and with the accounting relation between the financial and real economy' (Bezemer 2010, p. 678).

If you haven't yet studied economics, or you're in your early days of doing so at school or university, I hope this gives you pause: shouldn't mainstream economics also concern itself with finance and debt? Surely they are essential features of the economy? *Au contraire*, the mainstream long ago convinced itself that even money doesn't really affect the economy, and hence monetary phenomena – including money, banks and private debt – are omitted from Neoclassical models. One Neoclassical economist put it this way on Twitter:

> Most people who teach macro do it by leading people through simple models without money, so they understand exchange and production and trade, international and inter-temporal. You can even do banks without money [yes!]. And it's better to start there. Then later, study money as it superimposes itself and complicates things, giving rise to inflation, exchange rates, business cycles.

This statement was made in late 2020 – a dozen years *after* the failure of Neoclassical models to anticipate the crisis.

Why didn't mainstream economists change their beliefs about the significance of money in economics after their failure in 2007? Here, paradoxically, economics is little different to physics, in that significant change in physics does *not*, in general, occur because adherents of an old way of thinking are convinced to abandon it by an experiment whose results contradict their theory. Instead, these adherents continue to cling to their theory, despite the experimental evidence it has failed. Humans, it appears, are more wedded to their beliefs about reality – their 'paradigms', to use Thomas Kuhn's famous phrase (Kuhn 1970) – than reality itself. Science changed, not because these scientists changed their minds, but because they were replaced by new scientists who accepted the new way of thinking. As Max Planck put it:

a new scientific truth does not triumph by convincing its opponents and making them see the light, but rather because its opponents eventually die, and a new generation grows up that is familiar with it. (Planck 1949, pp. 33–4)

Here, economics is different, largely because economic 'experiments' are different to scientific ones, in that they are historical events, whereas scientific experiments are deliberate attempts to confirm a theory – some of which fail. The Michelson–Morley experiment attempted to measure the speed of the Earth relative to 'the aether', the medium that scientists then thought allowed light to travel through space. The experiment found that there was no discernible relative motion, which implied that the aether did not exist. This unexpected discovery led to the rejection of the aether theory, and ultimately the adoption of the Theory of Relativity. This experiment can be repeated at any time – and it has been repeated, with increasingly more sophisticated methods – and the result is always the same. There is no way of getting away from it and returning to a pre-Relativity science, and nor is there any desire to do so by post-Relativity physicists.

In economics, however, it *is* possible to get away from the failure of theory to play out as expected in reality. An event like the GFC occurs only once in history, and it cannot be reproduced to allow old and new theories to be tested against it. As time goes on, the event itself fades from memory. History can help sustain a memory, but economic history is taught at very few universities. Economists don't learn from history because they're not taught it in the first place.

The economy is also a moving target, whereas the physical world, relatively speaking, is a stationary one. When a clash between theoretical prediction and empirical results occurs in physics, the state of unease persists until a theoretical resolution is found. But in economics, though a crisis like the GFC can cause great soul searching when it occurs, the economy changes over time, and the focus of attention shifts.

Finally, unlike physicists, economists *do* want to return to pre-crisis economic theory. Events like the GFC upset the 'totem' that characterizes Neoclassical economics, the 'supply and demand' diagram (Leijonhufvud 1973),[4] in which the intersecting lines determine both equilibrium price and equilibrium quantity, and in which any government intervention necessarily makes things worse, by moving the market away from this equilibrium point. This image of a self-regulating and self-stabilizing market system is a powerful intellectual, and even emotional, anchor for mainstream economists.

These factors interact to make economics extremely resistant to fundamental change. In physics, anomalies like the clash between the results of the Michelson–Morley experiment and the predictions of pre-Relativity physics persist until the theory changes, because the experimental result is eternal. The anomaly doesn't go away, but the theory that it contradicted dies with the pre-anomaly scientists. Try as they might, they can't recruit adherents to the old theory amongst new students, because the students are aware of the anomaly, and won't accept any theory that doesn't resolve it.

In economics, anomalies are gradually forgotten, and new students can be recruited to preserve and extend the old beliefs, and to paper over anomalous phenomena. School and university economics courses become ways of reinforcing the Neoclassical paradigm, rather than fonts from which new theories spring in response to failures of the dominant paradigm.

In physics, intellectual crises are intense but, relatively speaking, short-lived. The crisis persists until a new theoretical breakthrough resolves it – regardless of whether that breakthrough persuades existing physicists (which as a rule, it doesn't). The 'anomaly', the empirical fact that fundamentally contradicts the existing paradigm, is like the grain of sand in an oyster that ultimately gives birth to a pearl: the irritation cannot be avoided, so it must be dealt with (Woit 2006).[5] It is the issue that believers in the existing paradigm know they cannot resolve – though it may take time for that realization to sink in, as various extensions of the existing paradigm are developed, each of which proves to be partially effective but inherently flawed. It is the thing young scientists are most aware of, the issue they want to be the one to resolve. As their lecturers who stick to the old paradigm age, the students take in the old ideas, but they are actively looking for where they are wrong, and how these contradictions might be resolved.

Once a solution is found, the protestations of the necessarily older, ageing, sometimes retired and often deceased champions of the previous paradigm mean nothing. Ultimately, all the significant positions in a university department are filled by scientists who are committed to the new paradigm. Then, as the new paradigm develops, it first undergoes a period of rapid extension, but ultimately confronts its own critical anomaly, and the science falls into crisis once more, as philosopher of science Thomas Kuhn (Kuhn 1970) explains.[6]

This is a punctuated path of development. It starts with the development of an initial paradigm by a great thinker, around whom a community of followers coalesces. They extend the core insights and thus form a new paradigm in that science. Initially, they enjoy a glorious period of the dance between observation and theory, where observations confirm and extend the paradigm. But finally, some prediction the theory makes is contradicted by observation. After a period of denial and dismay, the science settles into an unhappy peace: the paradigm is taught, but with less enthusiasm, the anomaly is noted, and the various within-paradigm attempts to resolve it are discussed. Then, out of somewhere, whether from a Professor (Planck) or a patents clerk (Einstein), a resolution comes. Rinse and repeat.

Those punctuations never occur in economics, and because the punctuations don't occur, neither does the kind of revolutionary change in the discipline that Kuhn vividly describes for physics and astronomy. *Economics is, therefore, not a science.* As Kuhn explains brilliantly, a real science goes through a process of paradigm change via a shift from what he calls 'normal science', to a scientific revolution triggered by a fundamental anomaly and resolved by a new paradigm, after which normal science resumes once more with the new paradigm. Economics has experienced many theoretical and empirical crises since the Neoclassical school became dominant in the 1870s, but none have resulted in a revolution to a new paradigm akin to the shift from Ptolemaic to Copernican astronomy.

An economic crisis, when it strikes, does disturb the mainstream. Their textbook advice – if the crisis is empirical rather than theoretical – is thrown out of the window by policymakers while the crisis lasts. Mainstream economists react defensively – which is not significantly different from what happens in a science. They can justify the extraordinary policy measures undertaken by the unexpected nature of the crisis, but then treat the contradiction the crisis poses for their theory as an aberration, which can be handled by admitting some modifications to peripheral aspects of the core theory. One example is the concept of 'bounded rationality' promoted by Joe Stiglitz (Stiglitz 2011, 2018). This can be invoked to say that, if everyone were strictly rational, then the problem would not have arisen, but because of 'bounded rationality', the general principle didn't apply and, in this instance, a deviation from policies recommended by the pure theoretical canon is warranted.

Minor modifications are made to the Neoclassical paradigm, but fundamental aspects of it remain sacrosanct. Again, this is comparable to the reactions to an anomaly by adherents to an existing paradigm in a science.

Over time, the crisis passes – whether that passing was aided or hindered by the advice of economists. A handful of economists break with the majority because of the anomaly, which is how heterodox economists are born. But the majority of students become as entranced as their teachers were by the fundamentally utopian Neoclassical vision of capitalism as a system without power, in which everyone receives their just rewards, and in which regulation and punishment are unnecessary, because The Market does it all. These new students replace their masters, and they continue to propagate the Neoclassical paradigm.

This is the first hurdle at which economics fails to be a science. The process Planck describes, of the death of adherents of the old (Neoclassical) paradigm resulting in them being replaced by a 'new generation' that is familiar with the 'new scientific truth', does not occur in economics.

The second hurdle is the political role of economic theory. The last genuine scientific revolution in economics occurred in the 1870s, when the Neoclassical took over from the Classical school of thought – the approach developed by Adam Smith (Smith 1776), extended by David Ricardo (Ricardo 1817) and commandeered by Marx (Marx 1867). Neoclassical economists imagine that their theories originated with Smith (Samuelson and Nordhaus 2010a, p. 5), but in fact Smith, Ricardo and Marx used an 'objective' theory of value that is completely at odds with Neoclassical theory. Ricardo explicitly rejected the utility-oriented, scarcity-based proto-Neoclassical economics of his contemporary Jean-Baptiste Say, declaring emphatically that:

> There are some commodities, the value of which is determined by their scarcity alone ... These commodities, however, form a very small part of the mass of commodities daily exchanged in the market ... says Adam Smith, '... It is natural that what is usually the produce of two days', or two hours' labour, should be worth double of what is usually the produce of one day's, or one hour's labour.' ...
> That this is really *the foundation of the exchangeable value of all things, excepting those which cannot be*

increased by human industry, is a doctrine of the utmost
importance in political economy; for from no source do
so many errors, and so much difference of opinion in
that science proceed, as from the vague ideas which are
attached to the word value. (Ricardo 1817, Chapter 1,
emphasis added)

The Classical school of thought had logical problems of
its own (Keen 1993a, 1993b; Steedman 1977), but a key
factor in its demise, and the rise of the Neoclassical school,
was that Marx turned the Classical approach into a critique
of capitalism itself (De Vroey 1975). Since then, the fact
that Neoclassical economics supports wealthy interests,
via its merit-based theory of income distribution, has
played a major role in cementing the dominant position of
Neoclassical economics. Well-funded 'thinktanks' promote
its analysis of capitalism, so that its analysis of the economy
dominates popular and political discourse on economics.
This ideological role of Neoclassical economics means that
it is defended vigorously, even when reality proves it to be
wildly wrong about the nature of capitalism itself.

These same factors isolate those economists who
refuse to ignore the empirical and theoretical failings of
Neoclassical economics, and who form rival paradigms
like Post Keynesian, Marxian, Austrian and Biophysical
Economics. These academics survive as marginalized
iconoclasts within the economics departments of leading
universities (like Ha Joon Chang and Tony Lawson
at Cambridge University), as leading academics in
Departments of Business or Management rather than
Economics (like Mariana Mazzucato at UCL's Faculty
of the Built Environment), or as lecturers in Economics
in low-ranked universities that prominent Neoclassicals
don't want to work in (such as the University of Western
Sydney in Australia, and Kingston University in the UK,
where I was respectively a Professor and Head of School).

Given this dominance of the Neoclassical paradigm
despite numerous crises, both empirical and logical

(Keen 2011), and the co-existence of incompatible rival paradigms, the discipline sits in a state of perpetual, understated and unresolved crisis. Neoclassical economics evolves over time, in ways that its adherents believe are scientific revolutions, but it is never replaced in the way that obsolete paradigms are replaced in science. Rival paradigms develop as well, but never lead to the discredited Neoclassical paradigm being displaced.

Perhaps you're thinking 'But what about the Keynesian Revolution?'. Keynes certainly saw his work as constituting a clear break with the Neoclassical orthodoxy – which he described as 'classical economics':

> I accuse the classical economic theory of being itself one of these pretty, polite techniques which tries to deal with the present by abstracting from the fact that we know very little about the future. (Keynes 1937, p. 215)

However, Keynes's revolutionary ideas were snuffed out by John Hicks, in a paper that purported to reach a reconciliation between 'Mr Keynes and the Classics' (Hicks 1937) by developing what became known as the IS-LM model.[7] Hicks interpreted Keynes as not revolutionary at all, but merely adding 'the Economics of Depression' to the existing Neoclassical toolkit:

> With this revision, Mr. Keynes takes a big step back to Marshallian orthodoxy, and his theory becomes hard to distinguish from the revised and qualified Marshallian theories, which, as we have seen, are not new. Is there really any difference between them, or is the whole thing a sham fight? Let us have recourse to a diagram. (Hicks 1937, p. 153)

Though he presented his model as 'a convenient synopsis of Keynesian theory', and it was accepted as such by the majority of economists, Hicks later admitted that it was a Neoclassical, 'general equilibrium' model he had sketched out 'before I wrote even the first of my papers on Keynes' (Hicks 1981, p. 140).

The gap between what this model alleged was Keynesian economics, and the actual economics of Keynes, was enormous, as can readily be seen by comparing Hicks's 'suggested interpretation' of Keynes, and Keynes's own 24-page summary of his economics in 'The General Theory of Employment' (Keynes 1937), which was published two months before Hicks's paper. The key passage in Keynes's summary of his approach – which reflects the accusation he levelled at 'classical economic theory' above – is the following:

> The theory can be summed up by saying that ... the level of output and employment as a whole depends on the amount of investment ... More comprehensively, aggregate output depends on the propensity to hoard, on the policy of the monetary authority, on ... *But of these several factors it is those which determine the rate of investment which are most unreliable, since it is they which are influenced by our views of the future about which we know so little.*
>
> This that I offer is, therefore, a theory of why output and employment are so liable to fluctuation. (Keynes 1937, p. 221, emphasis added)

Keynes's summary of his theory asserts that the level of investment depends primarily upon *investors' expectations of the future*, which are uncertain and 'unreliable'. Hicks completely ignored expectations – let alone uncertainty – and instead, modelled investment as depending upon the money supply and the rate of interest:

> This brings us to what, from many points of view, is the most important thing in Mr. Keynes' book. It is not only possible to show that a given supply of money determines a certain relation between Income and interest...; it is also possible to say something about the shape of the curve. It will probably tend to be nearly horizontal on the left, and nearly vertical on the right ...

> Therefore, … the special form of Mr. Keynes' theory
> becomes valid. A rise in the schedule of the marginal
> efficiency of capital only increases employment, and does
> not raise the rate of interest at all. We are completely out
> of touch with the classical world. (Hicks 1937, p. 154; see
> also Hicks 1935; 1981)[8]

The schism between Hicks's purported model of Keynes and Keynes's own views was so great that it gave rise to the key heterodox school of thought, 'Post Keynesian Economics'. So 'the Keynesian revolution' didn't happen, though Post Keynesians themselves have developed approaches to economics that are revolutionary (Eiteman 1947; Godley 1999; Goodwin 1967; Graziani 1989; Keen 2020b; Minsky 1977; Moore 1979; Sraffa 1926, 1960). But a revolution in mainstream economic thought, like the rejection of Ptolemy's earth-centric vision of the solar system and its total replacement by Copernicus's sun-centric vision, has not happened.

The above paints a bleak picture of the prospects of replacing Neoclassical economics with a fundamentally different and far more realistic paradigm. But there have been changes over time that make this more feasible now than it was at Keynes's time.

Foremost here is the development of the computer, and computer software that can easily handle large-scale dynamic and even evolutionary processes (Gooding 2014). These developments have occurred outside economics, and especially in engineering, physics and meteorology. There are limitations of the applicability of these techniques to economics, largely because of the fact that economics involves human behaviour rather than the interaction of unconscious objects, but these limitations distort reality far less than the Neoclassical fantasy that economic processes occur in or near equilibrium.[9]

The development of the Post Keynesian school of thought after the Great Depression is also crucial. There were strident critics of the Neoclassical mainstream before the Great Depression, such as Joseph Schumpeter and Thorstein Veblen (Schumpeter 1928; Veblen 1898, 1908, 1909), but there was no truly revolutionary school of economic thought.[10] The development of this heterodox school over the eight decades between the Great Depression and the GFC meant that, when that crisis struck, there were coherent explanations of it – indeed, prescient warnings of it (Godley 2001; Godley and Izurieta 2002; Godley and Wray 2000; Keen 1995, 2006, 2007) – that did not exist when Keynes attempted his revolution.

Modern Monetary Theory (MMT), which arose out of interactions between the entrepreneur Warren Mosler (Mosler 1998, 2010) and a group of Post Keynesian economists – primarily Randy Wray (Wray 1994, 1997, 1998), Stephanie Kelton (Bell 2000, 2001), Scott Fullwiler (Fullwiler 2003, 2005) and Bill Mitchell (Mitchell 1987, 1994; Mitchell and Mosler 2002; Mitchell and Watts 2002) – has also done something that has not been achieved since Keynes: it has made the public at large aware of a distinctly non-Neoclassical approach to economics. A non-Neoclassical economics book, Stephanie Kelton's *The Deficit Myth* (Kelton 2020), has become a best-seller, ranking in the top 300 on Amazon on its debut. MMT is challenging the stranglehold that the Neoclassical school has on public opinion, and their myriad protestations about MMT are a sign that they are, for once, worried about losing their dominance.

Similarly, non-Neoclassical scholars like Mariana Mazzucato (Mazzucato 2015, 2019), Bill Janeway (Janeway 2012) and Kate Raworth (Raworth 2017) have, if not broken the hold that the Neoclassical meme of 'supply and demand' has on how the public thinks about economics, at least shaken it by showing that there are alternative, and empirically grounded, ways to thinking about the public and private sector's roles in innovation, and the dependence of the economy on the environment. Statistically-oriented researchers like Schularick, Jordà, Taylor and Bezemer are analysing issues, such as the role of credit in macroeconomics, which are ignored by Neoclassical econometricians (Bezemer and Grydaki 2014; Jordà et al. 2011, 2019; Schularick and Taylor 2012; Zhang and Bezemer 2014). Some mathematicians have become aware of fundamental fallacies in economics, such as the timeless, 'ergodic' foundations of Neoclassical finance theory (Peters 2019; Peters and Gell-Mann 2016) and are actively working on alternative approaches (Costa Lima et al. 2014; Grasselli and Costa Lima 2012; Grasselli and Nguyen-Huu 2018).

Finally, social media has allowed student movements critical of Neoclassical economics to evolve, flourish and persist in a way that was impossible before the Internet. I led the first ever student revolt against Neoclassical economics, at Sydney University in 1973 (Butler et al. 2009).[11] This revolt succeeded, in that the University finally agreed to create a Department of Political Economy to house the dissidents, but the protest and its success were restricted to just one university in far-away Australia. French students established the 'Protest Against Autistic Economics' in 2000, which had somewhat more traction, but no changes in economics teaching occurred: its main legacy was an online journal called the *Real World Economic Review*.

The real breakthrough came with a protest by economics students at the University of Manchester[12] in the UK in 2012, in response to the failure of their teachers to take the GFC seriously in their macroeconomics courses. As they put it, 'The economics we were learning seemed separate from the economic reality that the world was facing, and devoid from the crisis that had made many of us interested in economics to begin with'. Their Post-Crash Economics movement in turn spawned the international Rethinking Economics campaign, which now has groups in about 100 universities across the world (you should join one, if you're not already a member), and inspired the Institute for New Economic Thinking to fund the Young Scholars' Initiative.

There are therefore students eager for approaches to economics that break away from the Neoclassical mainstream, methods of analysis which can easily supplant the dated equilibrium methods used by Neoclassical economics, and rival schools of thought with an intellectual tradition spanning almost a century, on which an alternative paradigm can be constructed. What we lack is a university system in which these conditions can foment a paradigm shift, as has occurred several times in physics in the last one and a half centuries, but not once in economics.

Fortunately, the GFC was such an extreme shock to the policy bodies around the world, which were and are still dominated by Neoclassical economists, that at least some of them – such as the OECD, which established the unit New Approaches to Economic Challenges (NAEC) in 2012 (see https://www.oecd.org/naec/) – have started to explore alternative approaches, including the application of ideas from other disciplines (largely physics, engineering and computer programming) to economics. Change is more likely to come from these institutions than from within academic economics itself, though even here, the alternative approaches experience hostility from entrenched Neoclassical economists.

There is also one negative factor that may finally force the change needed in economics, which is closer to the Reformation of a degenerate religion than a standard scientific revolution (Elliott 2017). Climate change is the dominant issue for the human species – and all other species – during the twenty-first century, and the work that Neoclassical economists have done on climate change is, in my considered opinion, the worst work they have ever done (Keen 2020a). And yet Neoclassical economists gave their highest accolade, the deceptively named 'Sveriges Riksbank Prize in Economic Sciences in Memory of Alfred Nobel', to the chief proponent of this work, William Nordhaus. When reality exposes how low grade and utterly misleading this work has been, the revulsion that policymakers and the public will feel at how they have been deceived by economists may finally terminate Neoclassical economics.

I don't want you to be on the wrong side of this stage in history. If you are a potential or current student of economics, I want to reach you before you embark on, or get too deeply into, a university course of study that will attempt to inculcate a near-religious belief in the Neoclassical paradigm, and that will drive you away if you can't accept it. I want you to arrive at university knowing of the modern methods of analysis that are commonplace in the sciences and engineering, but which have been excluded from economics by the hegemony of Neoclassical economics. Then, perhaps, there will be a chance for a real revolution in economics, and it can become, if not a fully-fledged science, then at least more like a science and less like a religion.

It's not possible to state ahead of time what the entire new paradigm will be, but the following features are fundamental. The new paradigm will:

- be fundamentally monetary, in contrast to the false, moneyless barter model that underlies Neoclassical economics;
- acknowledge that the economy is a complex system, not an equilibrium system;
- be consistent with the fundamental physics known as the Laws of Thermodynamics;
- be grounded in empirical realism, rather than the fantasy of 'as if' assumptions about reality; and
- be based on the techniques of system dynamics and related non-equilibrium analytic approaches.

I explore each of these theses in the following chapters. What follows is a Manifesto, both because it is a call for change in economics every bit as emphatic as Martin Luther's call for the reform of the Christian religion, and also because it states my own distinctive approach to economics. However, this approach has been guided by the genuine giants of economics, philosophy and mathematics who influenced me, and I hope I do them justice in both the text and the many references on which it is based.

Lastly, this book makes heavy use of the modelling program I have designed, which I named *Minsky* in honour of the great Post Keynesian economist Hyman Minsky. I encourage you to download *Minsky* yourself, and use it to run the models in this book as you read about them here. The *Minsky* program (which runs on Windows, Apple and Linux PCs), all the models in this book, and a free manual, *Modelling with Minsky*, are available at http://www.profstevekeen.com/minsky/.

2

Money matters

Most people who haven't studied economics expect economists to be experts on money. However, as noted in the
previous chapter, Neoclassical macroeconomics effectively
ignores banks, and private debt, and money. Neoclassical
economists justified this omission with the assertion that
banks – and their products, debt and money – were
largely irrelevant to macroeconomics. Ex-Federal Reserve
Chairman Ben Bernanke put it this way, when he dismissed
Irving Fisher's argument that the Great Depression was
caused by a process that Fisher termed 'debt-deflation':

> Fisher envisioned a dynamic process in which falling
> asset and commodity prices created pressure on nominal
> debtors, forcing them into distress sales of assets, which in
> turn led to further price declines and financial difficulties
> ... Fisher's idea was less influential in academic circles,
> though, *because of the counterargument that debt-deflation
> represented no more than a redistribution from one group
> (debtors) to another (creditors)*. Absent implausibly large
> differences in marginal spending propensities among the
> groups, it was suggested, *pure redistributions should have
> no significant macroeconomic effects*. (Bernanke 2000,
> p. 24, emphasis added)

By 'pure redistribution', what Bernanke meant is that, in the Neoclassical model of banking, lending and the repayment of debt transfer money from one group to another – from saver to borrower in the case of lending, and from borrower to saver in the case of repayment – without affecting the aggregate amount of money in use. Therefore, unless there is a substantial difference in the rate at which savers and borrowers spend, this model predicts that the macroeconomic impact of a substantial fall in the level of debt – a 'debt-deflation' – will be slight.

'Nobel Prize' recipient Paul Krugman elaborated on this argument in his *New York Times* column, where he has frequently promoted the 'Loanable Funds' model of banking (Krugman 2009, 2011a, 2011b, 2013, 2015a, 2015b). In this model, banks are intermediaries between 'more patient people' who want a return on their savings, and 'less patient people' who want to spend more than their incomes at some point in time:

> Think of it this way: when debt is rising, it's not the economy as a whole borrowing more money. It is, rather, a case of less patient people – people who for whatever reason want to spend sooner rather than later – borrowing from more patient people. (Krugman 2012, p. 147)

In this model, lending simply shuffles existing money from one set of people to another: banks take in deposits from some customers, and lend them out as loans to other customers. There is also no relationship between the level of private debt and the amount of money in the economy.

This description of how banks operate needs a separate explanation of how the amount of money in the economy changes, since behaviour in this model just changes the distribution of the existing stock of money.

In Neoclassical economics, money creation is primarily the province of the government, via what is known as 'Fractional Reserve Banking', or the 'Money Multiplier'. A bank, it is asserted, takes in deposits from savers, and then lends out a large fraction of these deposits to borrowers. This lending creates money in an iterative process involving several banks, not just one in isolation. The amount created is largely determined by the government via its central bank, and actions by banks (and the non-bank public) can only *reduce* the amount of money created, not increase it. Gregory Mankiw explains it in this way in his textbook *Macroeconomics*:

> If the Federal Reserve adds a dollar to the economy and that dollar is held as currency, the money supply increases by exactly one dollar. But ... if that dollar is deposited in a bank, and banks hold only a fraction of their deposits in reserve, the money supply increases by more than one dollar. As a result, to understand what determines the money supply under fractional reserve banking, we need to take account of the interactions among (1) the Fed's decision about how many dollars to create, (2) banks' decisions about whether to hold deposits as reserves or to lend them out, and (3) households' decisions about whether to hold their money in the form of currency or demand deposits. (Mankiw 2016, pp. 93–4)

There are three factors that determine the money supply in this model: the 'monetary base', which 'is directly controlled by the Federal Reserve'; the fraction of any bank deposits that banks hold on to, which 'is determined by the business policies of banks and the laws regulating banks', and the amount of money the public hold in cash versus the amount they deposit in banks.

The only point in this model at which banks have an active role is their capacity to hold a *higher* fraction of deposits as reserves than they are required to do by law, and the only impact this can have is to *reduce* the amount of money created (bank customers can also reduce the amount of money created by keeping more of their money as cash). The central bank therefore has the dominant role in determining the money supply, according to Neoclassical economics. For this reason, in his *Essays on the Great Depression*, Bernanke blamed the calamity of the Great Depression on the Federal Reserve itself:

> our analysis provides the clearest indictment of the Federal Reserve and US monetary policy. Between mid-1928 and the financial crises that began in the spring of 1931, the Fed not only refused to monetize the substantial gold inflows to the United States but actually managed to convert positive reserve inflows into negative growth in the M1 money stock. Thus Fed policy was actively destabilizing in the pre-1931 period ... our methods attribute a substantial portion of the worldwide deflation prior to 1931 to these policy decisions by the Federal Reserve. (Bernanke 2000, p. 111)[1]

In contrast, the Post Keynesian economist Hyman Minsky followed Irving Fisher (Fisher 1932, 1933), and blamed the Great Depression on the disequilibrium dynamics of private debt. Minsky combined Fisher's ideas with Keynes's to develop what he christened the 'Financial Instability Hypothesis' (Minsky 1963, 1975, 1977, 1978). Private debt, which Neoclassical economists ignore, was an essential component of Minsky's analysis of the instability of capitalism.

For rising debt to cause rising economic activity, there must be some mechanism by which rising debt boosts aggregate demand – in contrast to the Neoclassical argument that changes in the level of debt were 'pure redistributions' with 'no significant macroeconomic effects' (Bernanke 2000, p. 24). If Minsky was right, then the Neoclassical models of 'Loanable Funds' and 'Fractional Reserve Banking – Money Multiplier' must therefore be wrong: bank lending must somehow create money, and this must also increase aggregate demand.

Minsky and other Post Keynesian economists – and some policy economists in central banks as well (Holmes 1969) – have argued for many decades that these Neoclassical models are indeed false, and that banks create money when they lend (Fisher 1933; Fontana and Realfonzo

2005; Fullwiler 2013; Graziani 1989; Hudson 2004; Keen 1995; Minsky 1963, 1990; Minsky and Vaughan 1990; Moore 1979, 1988, 1997, 2001; Schumpeter 1934; Werner 2014a, 2014b). Their protestations were ignored by Neoclassical economists, but in 2014, no less an institution than The Bank of England sided with the Post Keynesians (Kumhof and Jakab 2015; Kumhof et al. 2015; McLeay et al. 2014a, 2014b),[2] and stated emphatically that the Neoclassical models of banking – 'Loanable Funds', 'Fractional Reserve Banking' and 'The Money Multiplier' – were false:

> *The reality of how money is created today differs from the description found in some economics textbooks*:
> • Rather than banks receiving deposits when households save and then lending them out, *bank lending creates deposits.*
> • In normal times, the central bank does not fix the amount of money in circulation, nor is central bank money 'multiplied up' into more loans and deposits. (McLeay et al. 2014a, p. 14, emphasis added)

The Bundesbank made a similar pronouncement in 2017:

> It suffices to look at the creation of (book) money as a set of straightforward accounting entries to grasp that money and credit are created as the result of complex interactions between banks, non-banks and the central bank. And *a bank's ability to grant loans and create money has nothing to do with whether it already has excess reserves or deposits at its disposal.* (Deutsche Bundesbank 2017, p. 13, emphasis added)

Neoclassical economists could not completely ignore these flat-out contradictions of their models of banking by establishment bodies like central banks, but rather than accepting the critique and abandoning their models, their reaction was defensive. For example, Krugman argued that the Bank of England's paper was nothing new – and therefore it did not challenge the relevance of the Loanable Funds model, even though the model itself was technically wrong:

> OK, color me puzzled. I've seen a number of people touting this Bank of England paper on how banks create money as offering some kind of radical new way of looking at the economy. And it is a good piece. *But it doesn't seem, in any important way, to be at odds with what Tobin wrote 50 years ago* ... Don't let monetary realism slide into monetary mysticism! (Krugman 2014, emphasis added)

Since then, Neoclassical textbooks have continued to teach the Loanable Funds and Fractional Reserve Banking models of banking (Mankiw 2016, pp. 71–6, 89–100),[3] as if there's nothing wrong with teaching factually incorrect models – as if the change from a model in which banks do not create money, to one in which they do, makes no difference to macroeconomics.

However, the fact that banks create money when they lend has an enormous impact on macroeconomics, and models which pretend that banks don't create money are utterly inaccurate models of capitalism. This can easily be illustrated using one of the new computer software tools I alluded to earlier: the Open Source (that is, free) 'system dynamics' program *Minsky*. You can download *Minsky* without charge from https://sourceforge.net/projects/minsky/. If you want to follow the argument in this chapter closely, I suggest you do so now – and also download the free companion book *Modelling with Minsky* from http://www.profstevekeen.com/minsky/.

2.1 Modelling the origins of fiat money in *Minsky*

Minsky is named after the great Post Keynesian economist Hyman Minsky, whom we'll meet again in the next chapter. *Minsky* the software was built to model money, which is something that, as noted above, Neoclassical economists have steadfastly refused to do properly.[4] Doing so properly has, on the other hand, been a core quest for Post Keynesian economists. A superb piece of logic by the Post Keynesian monetary theorist Augusto Graziani played a pivotal role in the development of *Minsky*, when he noted that three characteristics distinguished a monetary economy from a 'barter' system of exchange:

> (a) money has to be a token currency (otherwise it would give rise to barter and not to monetary exchanges);
> (b) money has to be accepted as a means of final settlement of the transaction (otherwise it would be credit and not money);
> (c) money must not grant privileges of seignorage to any agent making a payment.
> The only way to satisfy those three conditions is to have payments made by means of promises of a third agent, the typical third agent being nowadays a bank. (Graziani 1989, p. 3)

This meant that 'any monetary payment must therefore be a triangular transaction, involving at least three agents, the payer, the payee, and the bank' (Graziani 1989, p. 3). In place of the mythical barter-based Neoclassical model of trade (Graeber 2011),[5] in which two individuals, each with a commodity to exchange, try to work out a relative price between them – and where money is at best a specific commodity simply used as a convenient measuring stick, or 'numeraire' – this is a fundamentally monetary vision of capitalism. There is *one* person selling *one* commodity, another buying it with money, and the payment is effected by a transfer of a sum from the buyer's bank account – the bank's 'promise to pay' – to the seller's bank account. Therefore, to understand money, you must understand banking.

Banks themselves developed out of the double-entry bookkeeping system designed by accountants to keep track of financial commitments (Gleeson-White 2011; Graeber 2011). In double-entry bookkeeping, all transactions are recorded twice, once from the source account and once in the destination account. Accounts are also classified as assets, liabilities, or equity, following the rule that an entity's assets minus its liabilities equals its equity, or net worth.

Graziani's insight, coupled with the fundamental role of double-entry bookkeeping in banking, led to *Minsky*'s unique feature: its 'Godley Tables'. Named in honour of the pioneer of stock-flow consistent modelling Wynne Godley – who was also the first economist to explicitly warn that a serious economic crisis was inevitable in the early 2000s (Godley 2001; Godley and Izurieta 2002; Godley and Wray 2000) – Godley Tables build macroeconomic models based on monetary transactions, using double-entry bookkeeping.

Each column in a Godley Table represents the account of an institution or social class in a *Minsky* model, where that account must be either an asset, or a liability, or the difference between the two, the equity of that entity.[6] Since one entity's asset is another's liability,[7] each recording of an account as an asset requires its recording as a liability in another Godley Table for that other entity.

It's important to remember, as you read the following figures, that the entries are the *accounting record*, not the actual thing itself: for example, figure 2.1's model of commodity money shows the record of the amount of gold held by each of the butter, gun and coffee producers, and not the actual gold itself. Think of the entries as records in a spreadsheet file, rather than the things themselves, whether these be grams of gold in a vault, penny coins in your pocket, or electronic dollars stored in a bank database.

Each row in a Godley Table has two entries recording a specific type of transaction at the aggregate level for a macroeconomy – such as the payment of wages, interest on existing debt or the creation of new debt. The row *must* sum to zero – otherwise you have made an accounting error. Combined with the 'one person's asset is another person's liability' rule, this means that in a complete *Minsky* model, each transaction is recorded four times.

Minsky then uses Godley Tables to build an integrated, dynamic model, with the sum of the entries in each column determining the *rate of change* of the account that column represents. Since *Minsky* checks to ensure that each row is correct, a model involving possibly dozens of interlocking accounts can easily be constructed, and edited, with *Minsky* ensuring that the accounting – if not the model itself – is valid.

This method of modelling money is both remarkably simple and remarkably powerful. It can easily demonstrate the fallacies in the Neoclassical treatment of money, and banks, as mere intermediaries that can be omitted from macroeconomics.

An intermediary is an entity that makes a given process easier, but which isn't essential to the process itself. In this sense, Neoclassicals treat money as an intermediary to barter. If a butter producer wanted a gun (to protect his herd) while the gun producer wanted butter (to spread on his toast), and they knew each other, then a transaction between them could happen without money, at some agreed ratio of butter to guns. Money makes this much easier, partly by being a measuring stick, but more importantly, by eliminating the problem of the 'double coincidence of wants'. This is the dilemma that, for a direct exchange of guns for butter to occur, the producer of guns and the producer of butter must want each other's commodity. If the butter producer wants a gun, but the gun producer wants coffee, then the butter-for-guns trade is not going to occur.

In the Neoclassical story, money evolves from trade itself, when traders agree to use a specific commodity – preferably one that doesn't degrade, such as silver or gold – as the money commodity. With gold as the money commodity, the butter producer can sell her butter for gold, and use that gold to buy a gun, after which the gun producer uses the gold to buy coffee. Money thus allows trade to occur more easily, and expands the number of trades over what they would be in its absence.

Figure 2.1 shows this process using Godley Tables. The butter maker sells butter to the coffee maker for gold, and then uses this gold to buy the gun from the gun maker, who then buys coffee.

As noted earlier, Godley Tables classify all financial accounts as either assets, liabilities, or equity. This commodity-money world is one in which money (gold) is an asset to its holder, but a liability to no-one. None of the three agents shown in figure 2.1 have any liabilities, so their equity, in money terms, is precisely equal to their holdings of gold. The double-entry rules that apply to a monetary economy are irrelevant here.

In this world, people hold the money commodity not for its own sake, but for use as an intermediary in trade:

Butter

Flows ↓ / Stock Vars →	Asset	Liability	Equity	A-L-E
	$Gold_{Butter}$ ▼		▼ $Butter_{Equity}$	0
Initial Conditions	10		10	0
Sell Butter to Coffee Maker	$Butter^{Gold}_{Value}$		$Butter^{Gold}_{Value}$	0
Buy Gun	$-Gun^{Gold}_{Value}$		$-Gun^{Gold}_{Value}$	0

Coffee

Flows ↓ / Stock Vars →	Asset	Liability	Equity	A-L-E
	$Gold_{Coffee}$ ▼		▼ $Coffee_{Equity}$	0
Initial Conditions	100		100	0
Buy Butter	$-Butter^{Gold}_{Value}$		$-Butter^{Gold}_{Value}$	0
Sell Coffee	$Coffee^{Gold}_{Value}$		$Coffee^{Gold}_{Value}$	0

Guns

Flows ↓ / Stock Vars →	Asset	Liability	Equity	A-L-E
	$Gold_{Gun}$ ▼		▼ Gun_{Equity}	0
Initial Conditions	200		200	0
Sell Gun	Gun^{Gold}_{Value}		Gun^{Gold}_{Value}	0
Buy Coffee	$-Coffee^{Gold}_{Value}$		$-Coffee^{Gold}_{Value}$	0

Figure 2.1. Money enables the butter maker to buy a gun without the gun maker having to want butter. See http://www.profstevekeen.com/minsky/

it is held as a means to more easily convert commodities
the buyer has and doesn't want, into commodities she
hasn't got and does want. The clearest statement of this
was made by one of the true precursors of Neoclassical
economics – not Adam Smith, as many Neoclassicals
believe, but Jean-Baptiste Say:

> Every producer asks for money in exchange for his
> products, only for the purpose of employing that money
> again immediately in the purchase of another product; for
> we do not consume money, and it is not sought after in
> ordinary cases to conceal it: thus, when a producer desires
> to exchange his product for money, he may be considered
> as already asking for the merchandise which he proposes
> to buy with this money. *It is thus that the producers,
> though they have all of them the air of demanding money
> for their goods, do in reality demand merchandise for their
> merchandise.* (Say 1821, Chapter 18, emphasis added)

Neoclassical economists imagine that the evolution
from a commodity-money economy to a paper money
economy was enabled by a benevolent State. Gold is
heavy, and difficult to assay – is it 24 carat gold, or only
18 carat, or even worse, 'fool's gold' (iron sulfide)? The
State first steps in to simplify the process, by minting 'gold
coins of known purity and weight'. Then the State acts
as custodian for the public's holdings of gold, taking in
the physical gold and issuing members of the public with
certificates to acknowledge that they, and not the State,
are the ultimate owners of that gold:

> The next step is for the government to accept gold from
> the public in exchange for gold certificates – pieces of
> paper that can be redeemed for a certain quantity of gold.
> If people believe the government's promise to redeem the
> paper bills for gold, the bills are just as valuable as the
> gold itself. In addition, because the bills are lighter than
> gold (and gold coins), they are easier to use in transac-
> tions. Eventually, no one carries gold around at all, and

these gold-backed government bills become the monetary standard.

Finally, the gold backing becomes irrelevant. If no one ever bothers to redeem the bills for gold, no one cares if the option is abandoned. As long as everyone continues to accept the paper bills in exchange, they will have value and serve as money. Thus, the system of commodity money evolves into a system of fiat money. (Mankiw 2016, p. 84)

One critical aspect of this assumed evolution is that, as figure 2.1 shows, the asset the State holds that underpins the system is a commodity – gold – while the money in circulation is a promissory note – the promise to exchange the note for physical gold if the note holder demands it. The asset is thus a physical thing, while the liability is a promise, recorded on a piece of paper. This assumed situation is shown in figure 2.2. We are now in a Neoclassical version of monetary economy, where to trade, people exchange the State's 'promise to redeem the paper bills for gold' – the State's liability to the public. From now on, the rule of double-entry bookkeeping, that one entity's asset is another's liability, applies. In this case, the promissory notes held by the butter, coffee and gun producers are all liabilities of the State.

With the perspective on money that its role is simply to facilitate the exchange of commodities, it makes sense to abstract from it altogether in economics – hence the treatment of money in Neoclassical economics as a 'veil over barter'. Money is only introduced in mainstream economics when explaining inflation, which is blamed on the currency issuer creating too much money, too quickly, relative to the real rate of growth of the economy. This was the key conclusion of one of the most influential papers in economics, Milton Friedman's 'The Optimum Quantity of Money' (Friedman 1969), in which he introduced the infamous concept of 'helicopter money'.

Far be it from me to accuse Friedman of being glib and misleading,[8] but this paper was as incomplete as it was

State

Flows ↓ / Stock Vars →	Asset	Liability			Equity	A-L-E
	$Gold_{State}$ ▼	$Money_{Butter}$ ▼	$Money_{Coffee}$ ▼	$Money_{Gun}$ ▼	$State_{Equity}$	0
Initial Conditions	310	10	100	200	0	0
Sell Butter to Coffee Maker		$Butter^{Gold}_{Value}$	$-Butter^{Gold}_{Value}$			0
Buy Gun		$-Gun^{Gold}_{Value}$		Gun^{Gold}_{Value}		0
Sell Coffee			$Coffee^{Gold}_{Value}$	$-Coffee^{Gold}_{Value}$		0

Guns

Flows ↓ / Stock Vars →	Asset	Liability	Equity	A-L-E
	$Money_{Gun}$ ▼		▼ Gun_{Equity}	0
Initial Conditions	200		200	0
Sell Gun	Gun^{Gold}_{Value}		Gun^{Gold}_{Value}	0
Buy Coffee	$-Coffee^{Gold}_{Value}$		$-Coffee^{Gold}_{Value}$	0

Butter

Flows ↓ / Stock Vars →	Asset	Liability	Equity	A-L-E
	$Money_{Butter}$ ▼		▼ $Butter_{Equity}$	0
Initial Conditions	10		10	0
Sell Butter to Coffee Maker	$Butter^{Gold}_{Value}$		$Butter^{Gold}_{Value}$	0
Buy Gun	$-Gun^{Gold}_{Value}$		$-Gun^{Gold}_{Value}$	0

Coffee

Flows ↓ / Stock Vars →	Asset	Liability	Equity	A-L-E
	$Money_{Coffee}$ ▼		▼ $Coffee_{Equity}$	0
Initial Conditions	100		100	0
Buy Butter	$-Butter^{Gold}_{Value}$		$-Butter^{Gold}_{Value}$	0
Sell Coffee	$Coffee^{Gold}_{Value}$		$Coffee^{Gold}_{Value}$	0

Figure 2.2. The State as the conduit for fiat money transfers where money is the State's liability and physical gold its asset. See http://www.profstevekeen.com/minsky/

influential. The fanciful vision of a helicopter dispensing dollar bills was not at all integrated with the initial section of the paper, in which there was already $1,000 of currency in circulation. Where did this money come from? Friedman assumed that this currency had already been issued by a fiat currency authority:

> All money consists of strict fiat money, i.e., pieces of paper, each labelled 'This is one dollar.' (Friedman 1969, p. 3)

He provided no history of the money, though, in his telling, these notes had existed 'long enough for the society to have reached a state of equilibrium' (Friedman 1969, p. 3). Why were the notes used by the community? In keeping with Neoclassical convention, his explanation emphasized its *voluntary* use by people to avoid barter's key weakness:

> Why, in this simple, hypothetical society, should people want to hold money? The basic reason is to serve as a

medium of circulation, or temporary abode of purchasing power, in order to avoid the need for the famous 'double coincidence' of barter. (Friedman 1969, p. 3)

But why were these notes used, and not any others? And why were the notes suddenly dropped from the helicopter also trusted:

> Let us suppose now that one day a helicopter flies over this community and drops an additional $1,000 in bills from the sky, which is, of course, hastily collected by members of the community. (Friedman 1969, pp. 4–5)

The only way to give this fiction some real-world substance is that the 'helicopter' must be owned by the same authority that had previously created the existing 1,000 $1 bills – otherwise, the notes would have been counterfeit, and this dropping of new 'dollar bills' from the sky would have been an act of forgery. Therefore, to make Friedman's model internally consistent, the fiat currency issuer *has* to be incorporated into the model. To make the model more than just a piece of armchair theorizing, we have to situate it in history. Here, the 'fiat money evolved from commodity money' story gives way to something both more realistic and more colourful.

Harvard Law Professor Christine Desan gives the example of the re-invention of fiat currencies in England after the fifth-century exit of the Roman Empire, which led to the collapse of commerce in this then-primitive backwater of Europe (Desan 2015). Fiat money – in the form of coin rather than paper – was later created by the military rulers of the many Kingdoms of pre-medieval England. A coin, minted with the King's likeness – Desan singles out Offa, the eighth-century King of Mercia, as a particularly good example – became a way of enabling commerce within the realm he controlled (Desan 2015, pp. 42–57). What gave the coin value was not the commodity it contained (the coin was valued at more than the value of the silver from which it was made), but

the Kingdom itself, which was carved out by the force
of the coin as much as by the force of the sword. What
enforced the use of the coin was both its creation by the
Kingdom, and its requirement that taxes had to be paid in
coin – where these taxes replaced a previous practice of
forced appropriation. Desan notes that the Neoclassical
story, in which independent traders collectively agree to
use a specific commodity as money, is fanciful, because 'it
is so difficult to understand how people who are engaged
only in bipolar exchanges can create a term for value that
is shared among them all'. Instead, the historical record
shows that:

> rulers chose to make the basic unit of account – the penny –
> out of silver. That choice gave silver a price ... The 'price' of
> silver was tied, by definition, to the value of the tribute or
> tax obligation: pennies made by the mint were the tokens
> used by the king to pay for resources advanced to him. At
> the time the tax was due, each penny carried value towards
> extinguishing the tax obligation. (Desan 2015, p. 58)

Given the State-created money token's use in paying
taxes, 'the tokens invited use as a mode of payment in
private deals as well' (Desan 2015, p. 58). In the real
world, therefore, money emerged as a creature of the State
(Knapp 1924), and was backed not by any commodity, but
by the power and authority of the government that issued
the coins. Also, contrary to the arguments of critics of fiat
money – who rail against the fact that fiat is backed by
nothing, and claim that this undermines commerce – the
creation of fiat money dramatically *expanded* commerce
in these post-Roman and pre-Medieval Kingdoms.

Therefore, to make Friedman's cash economy example
passably realistic, the minimal elements needed are the
initial creation of 1,000 penny coins by the State, the
State's spending of these coins into the economy, the use
of this currency in transactions, and finally, the taxing of
individuals by the State, to enforce the continued use of
the currency.

Creation of coins requires a Mint, which is owned by the government – which, in this historical hypothetical, is King Offa. The King authorizes the minting of coins by the Mint on behalf of his Treasury. This ushers in a totally different kind of money than the Neoclassical fantasy, as illustrated in figure 2.2, of a fiat currency as the State's liability, backed by a physical commodity as the State's asset. Instead, in this real-world historical example, the asset and the liability were *the same thing, and owned by the same entity*: one-penny coins, minted by one wing of government – the Mint – on behalf of another wing – the Treasury.

When these coins are recorded in the Godley Tables in figure 2.3, they appear as an asset of the Mint (the leftmost column in the first table), and a liability of the Treasury (the middle column in the second table). The minting process thus creates an asset of 1,000 pennies for the Mint, and a liability of 1,000 pennies for the Treasury. The two cancel out at the aggregate level of the government – since the Mint and the Treasury are both owned by the King. If the coins are immediately issued to the Treasury by the Mint, then the equity of both the Mint and the Treasury remain at zero throughout as the 1,000 coins are minted (this process is explained in detail in the free companion book *Modelling with Minsky*). Only as the coins are spent by the Treasury is money created in the Kingdom itself, and as they are spent by the Treasury, it goes into negative equity with respect to the Mint, as its holdings of coins are less than its 'debt' in coins.

This enables the government to create money 'out of nothing' – in the sense that no commodity is needed to back the coins. However, they are backed by the formidable power of the State that created them. Money does not outlive the State itself, but it prevails as long as the State that issued it.

Figure 2.3 shows the money-making process in sequential order (though the processes occur contemporaneously, and are modelled as such in *Minsky*):

- The Mint creates the coins;
- The Mint gives the coins to the Treasury;
- The Treasury spends the coins to procure goods from lords and peasants, where the purchase replaced the pre-monetary practice of compulsory acquisition at the point of a sword;
- The coins are then used by lords to pay peasants to produce output, which is sold to both lords and peasants, and the government; and
- Finally, coins are taxed from the lords and peasants by the Treasury.

As in history, so in this model: once the coins are in the hands of the public, they can be used for inter-personal

Mint

Flows ↓ / Stock Vars →	Asset $Coins_{Mint}$ ▼	Liability $Coins_{Treasury}$ ▼	$Coins_{Lords}$ ▼	$Coins_{Peasants}$ ▼	Equity $Mint_{Equity}$	A-L-E
Initial Conditions	0	0	0	0	0	0
Create coins	$Mint_{Coins}$				$Mint_{Coins}$	0
Give Coins to Treasury		$Issue_{Coins}$			$-Issue_{Coins}$	0
Spend on Peasants		$-Spend_{Peasants}$		$Spend_{Peasants}$		0
Spend on Lords		$-Spend_{Lords}$	$Spend_{Lords}$			0
Hire Peasants			$-Wages$	$Wages$		0
Peasants Consume			$Consume_{Peasants}$	$-Consume_{Peasants}$		0
Tax Peasants		$Tax_{Peasants}$		$-Tax_{Peasants}$		0
Tax Lords		Tax_{Lords}	$-Tax_{Lords}$			0

Treasury

Flows ↓ / Stock Vars →	Asset $Coins_{Treasury}$ ▼	Liability $Coins_{Mint}$ ▼	Equity $Treasury_{Equity}$	A-L-E
Initial Conditions	0	0	0	0
Create coins		$Mint_{Coins}$	$-Mint_{Coins}$	0
Give Coins to Treasury	$Issue_{Coins}$		$Issue_{Coins}$	0
Spend on Lords	$-Spend_{Lords}$		$-Spend_{Lords}$	0
Spend on Peasants	$-Spend_{Peasants}$		$-Spend_{Peasants}$	0
Tax_{Lords}	Tax_{Lords}		Tax_{Lords}	0
Tax Peasants	$Tax_{Peasants}$		$Tax_{Peasants}$	0

Lords

Flows ↓ / Stock Vars →	Asset $Coins_{Lords}$ ▼	Liability	Equity ▼ $Lords_{Equity}$	A-L-E
Initial Conditions	0		0	0
Hire Peasants	$-Wages$		$-Wages$	0
Peasants Consume	$Consume_{Peasants}$		$Consume_{Peasants}$	0
Spend on Lords	$Spend_{Lords}$		$Spend_{Lords}$	0
Tax_{Lords}	$-Tax_{Lords}$		$-Tax_{Lords}$	0

Peasants

Flows ↓ / Stock Vars →	Asset $Coins_{Peasants}$ ▼	Liability	Equity ▼ $Peasants_{Equity}$	A-L-E
Initial Conditions	0		0	0
Peasants Consume	$-Consume_{Peasants}$		$-Consume_{Peasants}$	0
Hire Peasants	$Wages$		$Wages$	0
Spend on Peasants	$Spend_{Peasants}$		$Spend_{Peasants}$	0
Tax Peasants	$-Tax_{Peasants}$		$-Tax_{Peasants}$	0

Figure 2.3. Modelling the initiation of a monetary economy in *Minsky*. See http://www.profstevekeen.com/minsky/

trade: the quite literal *making of money* by the State, as Desan put it, enabled the market to flourish. Figure 2.4 shows a simulation of this model (which is explained in detail in the free online companion book *Modelling in Minsky*).

Two essential aspects of this primordial fiat money creation process are firstly, that coins must be spent into the economy before they can be taxed back to the Treasury, and secondly, that this process requires the State to go into negative equity, while the private sector achieves precisely the same magnitude of positive equity. These aspects of this model are both consistent with what is called 'Modern Monetary Theory' today (Mosler 2010). Known by its initials MMT, it also asserts that today, government spending precedes taxation, and that what we call government debt is in fact the mirror image of the money created by the State.

The first point should be obvious in this model: spending by the Treasury is necessary before it can tax, because without the spending, there would be no coins in the economy, and therefore no monetary income to tax. As Stephanie Kelton asserts in *The Deficit Myth* (Kelton 2020), the government spends first, and taxes later. This remains contentious in political discourse today, because we are so far removed from the initial act of money creation by the State. But when one goes back to that point in time, as Desan does in *Making Money* (Desan 2015) and we have done here in this *Minsky* model, the point is obvious: the first act of taxation has to occur after the first act of spending, because before the State spends, there is no money in circulation to be taxed.

The second point is more challenging to grasp, but is also consistent with MMT's assertion that government debt today is the mirror image of the fiat money that accumulated government spending in excess of taxation has created. In this *Minsky* model, the negative equity of the State is in fact identical to the amount of money created by the State (see figure 2.4).

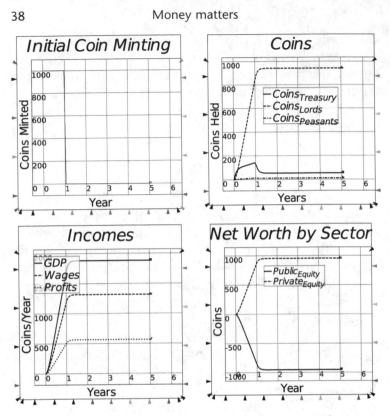

Figure 2.4. Growth of coins and the economy from an initial minting of 1,000 coins. See http://www.profstevekeen.com/minsky/

In this model, the account $Coins_{Mint}$ is simultaneously the record of an asset of the Mint, and a liability of the Treasury. After the Mint has given the coins to the Treasury, and before the Treasury spends, the Treasury's liabilities (the coins given to it by the Mint, $Coins_{Mint}$) equal its assets (the coins in its possession, $Coins_{Treasury}$), so that its equity is zero. As the Treasury spends, the amount it 'owes' the Mint in coins remains constant, but the number of coins in its possession falls as they are distributed to lords and peasants. The decline in the Treasury's equity precisely equals the rise in the equity of the lords and peasants, since each penny spent by the Treasury ends up either in the lords' possession or the peasants'. The Treasury's 'debt' to the Mint, in other words, is precisely equal to the amount of money in the economy. The Treasury going into debt to the Mint is one side of the process that creates money: the other is spending by the Treasury to buy (rather than appropriate) goods and services from the lords and peasants.

This leads to a rather remarkable inference: if Friedman had modelled his hypothetical monetary economy properly rather than glibly, he, and not Warren Mosler, would have invented Modern Monetary Theory. Instead, Friedman invented 'Monetarism' – the argument that 'inflation is always and everywhere a monetary phenomenon', and that therefore 'There is one and only one cure for inflation: to reduce the rate of monetary growth' (Friedman 1983, pp. 46, 50).

There are superficial similarities between Monetarism and Modern Monetary Theory, in that both attribute money creation to government action, and both assert that a government which pushes economic activity too high by creating too much money will cause inflation. However, behind these points of agreement lie utterly different visions of how the government creates money, and how its behaviour interfaces with the private sector. To evaluate these opposing views, we have to consider the modern system of fiat money.

2.2 Modelling modern fiat money in *Minsky*

Neoclassical textbooks assert that the government borrows from the public in order to finance its activities, that government activity 'crowds out' private, and that government debt burdens future generations:

> When a government spends more than it collects in taxes, it has a budget deficit, *which it finances by borrowing from the private sector* or from foreign governments. The

accumulation of past borrowing is the government debt. (Mankiw 2016, p. 555, emphasis added)

government borrowing reduces national saving and crowds out capital accumulation ... Many economists have criticized this increase in government debt as imposing an unjustifiable burden on future generations. (Mankiw 2016, pp. 556–7)

In the modern world, most money is in the form of bank deposits rather than coins or notes, and therefore money is primarily in the form of deposits in private banks. For simplicity, I leave cash out of the models in this section.

Bank deposits are liabilities of the private banking sector, rather than liabilities of the modern equivalent of Offa's Mint, the central bank. The government's interface with the private sector is therefore not direct, as in the model of Offa's coin-issuing Mint, but indirect, via private bank reserves, which are an asset of the private banks and a liability of the central bank.

Figure 2.5 shows the basic monetary operations of today's fiat-money system. The core operations are all visible in the first Godley Table, for the private banks:

- Government spending on the public (either via purchases of goods or direct income support);
- Taxing the public;
- Selling bonds to the financial sector to cover the gap between spending and taxation;
- Treasury paying interest on those bonds;
- The central bank buying some of those bonds off financial entities in 'open market operations';
- Banks selling Treasury Bonds to the non-bank private sector; and
- Treasury paying interest on those bonds to the public.

Several facts about government financing can be deduced from figure 2.5 that are the opposite of conventional beliefs – conventional beliefs which originate with

Private Banks

Flows ↓ / Stock Vars →	Asset		Liability	Equity	A-L-E
	Reserves	$Bonds_{Banks}$	Deposits	$Banks_{Equity}$	
Initial Conditions	0	0	0	0	0
Government Spending	Spend		Spend		0
Government Taxation	-Tax		-Tax		0
Treasury Bond sales to Banks	$-Sell_{Bonds}^{Banks}$	$Sell_{Bonds}^{Banks}$			0
Interest on Bonds to Banks	$Interest_{Bonds}^{Banks}$			$Interest_{Bonds}^{Banks}$	0
Sell Bonds to Central Bank	$Sell_{Bonds}^{CB}$	$-Sell_{Bonds}^{CB}$			0
Sell Bonds to Public		$-Sell_{Bonds}^{Public}$	$-Sell_{Bonds}^{Public}$		0
Interest on Bonds to Public	$Interest_{Bonds}^{Public}$		$Interest_{Bonds}^{Public}$		0

Central Bank

Flows ↓ / Stock Vars →	Asset		Liability		Equity	A-L-E
	$Bonds_{CB}$	$Loans_{Treasury}^{CB}$	Reserves	Treasury	CB_{Equity}	
Initial Conditions	0	0	0	0	0	0
Interest on Bonds to Banks			$Interest_{Bonds}^{Banks}$	$-Interest_{Bonds}^{Banks}$		0
Interest on Bonds to Public			$Interest_{Bonds}^{Public}$	$-Interest_{Bonds}^{Public}$		0
Treasury Bond sales to Banks			$-Sell_{Bonds}^{Banks}$	$Sell_{Bonds}^{Banks}$		0
Sell Bonds to Central Bank	$Sell_{Bonds}^{CB}$		$Sell_{Bonds}^{CB}$			0
Government Spending			Spend	-Spend		0
Government Taxation			-Tax	Tax		0
Borrow from Central Bank		$Lend_{Treasury}^{CB}$		$Lend_{Treasury}^{CB}$		0

Treasury

Flows ↓ / Stock Vars →	Asset	Liability				Equity	A-L-E
	Treasury	$Bonds_{Banks}$	$Bonds_{CB}$	$Bonds_{Public}$	$Loans_{Treasury}^{CB}$	$Treasury_{Equity}$	
Initial Conditions	0	0	0	0	0	0	0
Interest on Bonds to Banks	$-Interest_{Bonds}^{Banks}$					$-Interest_{Bonds}^{Banks}$	0
Interest on Bonds to Public	$-Interest_{Bonds}^{Public}$					$-Interest_{Bonds}^{Public}$	0
Treasury Bond sales to Banks	$Sell_{Bonds}^{Banks}$	$Sell_{Bonds}^{Banks}$					0
Government Spending	-Spend					-Spend	0
Government Taxation	Tax					Tax	0
Sell Bonds to Central Bank		$-Sell_{Bonds}^{CB}$	$Sell_{Bonds}^{CB}$				0
Sell Bonds to Public		$-Sell_{Bonds}^{Public}$		$Sell_{Bonds}^{Public}$			0
Borrow from Central Bank	$Lend_{Treasury}^{CB}$				$Lend_{Treasury}^{CB}$		0

Public

Flows ↓ / Stock Vars →	Asset		Liability	Equity	A-L-E
	Deposits	$Bonds_{Public}$		$Public_{Equity}$	
Initial Conditions	0	0		0	0
Government Spending	Spend			Spend	0
Government Taxation	-Tax			-Tax	0
Sell Bonds to Public	$-Sell_{Bonds}^{Public}$	$Sell_{Bonds}^{Public}$			0
Interest on Bonds to Public	$Interest_{Bonds}^{Public}$			$Interest_{Bonds}^{Public}$	0

Figure 2.5. The fundamental monetary operations of the government. See http://www.profstevekeen.com/minsky/

Neoclassical economists, and are promulgated in their textbooks, such as Mankiw's *Macroeconomics* (Mankiw 2016), as cited earlier.

Firstly, Neoclassicals allege that the government must borrow from the public to finance any excess of government spending over taxation. Figure 2.5 shows that this belief is the exact opposite of the truth. When government spending exceeds taxation (when *Spend* is greater than *Tax* in figure 2.5) then the amount of money in the private sector *increases* by the same amount: government spending increases the *Deposits* of the non-bank, non-government sector of the economy. This means that the banking sector's liabilities to the non-bank private sector rise, and this is matched by an identical increase in the banking sector's assets of *Reserves*. Since both the assets and the liabilities of the banking sector have risen, and money is the sum of the liabilities of the banking sector,[9] then *the deficit has created money* (Kelton 2020).[10] The government doesn't need to borrow what it has already created.

What about the sale of Treasury Bonds to the banking sector? Isn't that borrowing? Technically yes, because Treasury Bonds are a debt of the government to the holder of those bonds. But where does the banking sector get the funds it uses to buy these bonds? The real-world process is more complicated,[11] but fundamentally, as well as creating additional money (when *Spend* is greater than *Tax* in figure 2.5) the deficit creates an identical amount of reserves: they are the additional asset that matches the additional liabilities that net government spending on the public creates for the banking sector.

Reserves are an asset that normally earns no interest. So, when the government then offers to sell Treasury Bonds equal to the size of the deficit, it is presenting the banking sector with an offer to convert non-income-earning reserves into income-earning Treasury Bonds. This is one reason why every sale of US Treasury Bonds has been not merely successful, but oversubscribed: an auction of Treasury Bonds is an offer to convert a non-income-earning gift (the additional reserves created by the deficit) into an income-earning one (Treasury Bonds). Of course, the banking sector takes advantage of that offer.

What would happen if the Treasury didn't sell the bonds – so that all the bond-related flows in figure 2.5 would not exist? Money creation would still occur, because, in that case, the only entries in the liabilities side of the banking sector's accounts would be *Spend minus Tax*: the deficit itself creates money, regardless of whether or not bonds are sold to cover the deficit. The consequences of not selling bonds therefore lies elsewhere in the financial system.

Without the bond sales, the only guaranteed flows into and out of the Treasury's account at the central bank are *Tax minus Spend* – the same terms as for the creation of money, but with the opposite sign – see the third Godley Table in figure 2.5. Therefore, the impact of the government not selling bonds equal to the deficit each year would be that, with sustained deficits over time, the Treasury's deposit account at the central bank would go negative – it would turn into an overdraft account.

For a private entity, an overdraft at a private bank means a much higher interest rate than on a standard loan on the negative balance in its deposit account, limits on how high the overdraft can be, other possibly punitive measures, and the prospect, if the overdraft gets too large, of bankruptcy. But for the Treasury, there are no such consequences, since the Treasury is the effective owner of the central bank. In some countries, the Treasury doesn't have to pay interest on Treasury Bonds owned by the central bank; in others, it is required by law to pay interest to the central bank on any loans, including overdrafts. But in all countries, the profits of the central bank are remitted to the Treasury – so in effect the Treasury pays zero interest on its 'debt' to the central bank. There are effectively no consequences for the Treasury from having an overdraft at the central bank.

All bond sales do is enable the Treasury to avoid an overdraft, by keeping its central bank account positive (or at least non-negative). Most governments have passed laws requiring their Treasury to not be in overdraft to their central bank – though these laws were waived by some countries during the Covid-19 crisis. New laws, based on a realistic appreciation of the role of government money creation in a well-functioning economy, could enable the Treasury to always run an overdraft – or let it run up a debt to the central bank – obviating the need to sell bonds at all.

What about the interest on Treasury Bonds? That can be paid by the Treasury borrowing from the central bank, and thus adding to a loan on which it effectively pays zero interest – see the final line on the second and third Godley Tables in figure 2.5. This is the government *being in debt to itself*, and only for the *interest* it pays on the bonds it has sold.

The central bank also does not 'monetize' the government deficit when it buys Treasury Bonds off the banking sector. This common expression[12] is simply wrong, because the deficit is already 'monetized', since the deficit itself creates money when it increases the liabilities of the banking sector (*Deposits*) and the assets (*Reserves*). Central bank purchases of Treasury Bonds from the banking sector undo the effect of the Treasury selling those bonds to the banking sector in the first place: they replace income-earning assets in the banking sector's portfolio (Treasury Bonds) with non-income-earning ones (reserves). The banks wouldn't do the trade if they didn't make a trading profit (which is not included in the simple model in figure 2.5), but the end result is they end up with a lower income stream, since they no longer get the interest the Treasury pays on those bonds.

The only aspect of bond sales that affects the money supply is the sales of bonds by the banks to the non-bank private sector (shown as the second last row of the final Godley Table in figure 2.5), and this destroys money, rather than either creating it, or providing money to the government for it to spend. When banks sell Treasury Bonds to non-banks, the deposits of the non-banks fall, as do the bank's own assets of bonds. This destroys money: the public is exchanging instantly accessible money for slightly less liquid interest-earning bonds. Rather than such sales being a source of revenue for the government, they are a source of trading profits for the banks,[13] and a way to reduce the spending power of the public.

Where does the public get the money to buy these bonds? As with the funds banks use to buy bonds on the asset side of their ledger, the funds the public use are created by the deficit itself. So bond sales by private banks to the public reduce the amount of money created by the deficit, and if banks sold 100 per cent of the bonds that way, the deficit would not create money – but the public would have financial assets (the bonds) equivalent to the deficit.

This realistic perspective on government spending upends the conventional wisdom of Neoclassical economics. The government does not 'borrow from the private sector' when it runs a deficit. Instead, a deficit creates 'debt-free' money for the private sector. The deficit increases private savings, rather than reducing them, as Mankiw alleges. By providing an alternative 'debt-free' source of new money, government deficits thus make borrowing from private banks by households and firms less appealing – an issue we'll consider later in this chapter. Deficits also provide the private banks with a guaranteed source of income in the form of interest on government bonds. This could make them less likely to want to sell speculative financial assets to the non-bank private sector, and more likely to finance productive investment instead (one lives in hope).

Therefore, far from government deficits 'burdening future generations', *they enrich current generations monetarily*.[14] Any impact on future generations depends on the economic and political consequences of the spending which generates the deficit, and they can be substantially beneficial to the private sector, rather than deleterious. Consider, for example, the enormous deficits of up to 25 per cent of GDP, and the resulting trebling of government debt (from 38 per cent to 118 per cent of GDP) caused by government spending during the Second World War (see figure 2.6). Without that deficit – which, as we have seen above, was funded by fiat money creation, not by borrowing from the public or the banks – and corresponding ones for its allies (the UK's deficit hit 44 per cent of GDP in 1941), the Axis powers could well have won the war.

Deficits of that scale rapidly increased the government debt to GDP ratio, to 118 per cent of GDP – the highest in America's history before Covid-19. According to Mankiw and almost all Neoclassical economists, this should have placed an enormous burden on the 'future generation' that

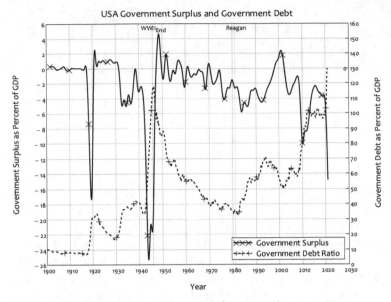

Figure 2.6. US government debt and deficits over the past 120 years

followed the wartime one. So how did this unfortunate cohort fare?

I speak, of course, of the Baby Boomers. Born between 1946 and 1964, as children, they were probably the most privileged and spoilt generation in human history. Far from suffering pain as their parents paid back the enormous government debts accumulated during the Second World War, their time in the nurseries of school and university coincided with the 'Golden Age of Capitalism' (Marglin and Schor 1992) between 1950 and 1973, when their parents experienced high growth, low unemployment, low inflation, and – in an apparent paradox – a *falling* government debt-to-GDP ratio, while the budget was normally in deficit (see table 2.1). If that's being burdened, then please, bring it on.

The Baby Boomers' woes only began *after* 1973, when inflation and unemployment both rose at much the same time (see figure 2.7). Normally, when inflation rose, unemployment fell, which appeared to vindicate

Table 2.1. Economic performance of major periods in post-Second World War USA

| Period | Years | Economic indicators | | | | Debt | | | |
| | | Annual average % | | | | Public | | Private | |
		Growth	Unemployment	Inflation	Deficit	Start	End	Start	End
Golden Age	1950–1973	4.15	4.77	2.48	0.69	87.4	40.4	55.8	94.3
Post-War	1945–2020	2.58	5.7	3.68	2.26	109	104	40.1	150
Post-Golden	1973–2020	2.26	6.28	3.94	3.10	40.4		94.3	
Post-GFC	2008–2020	1.6	6.5	1.8	4.9	58.2		166	

the 'inflation–unemployment trade-off' interpretation of the 'Phillips curve', the statistical relationship between inflation and unemployment (in Britain between 1861 and 1957) that had been identified by the New Zealand economist Bill Phillips (Phillips 1958).[15]

When inflation rose from 2.7 per cent in mid-1972 to a post-war high of 12.4 per cent in 1975, unemployment also fell for a while – from 6 per cent at the end of 1971 to 4.6 per cent in October 1973. But unemployment then also began to rise – from 4.6 per cent in October 1973 to a post-war peak of 9 per cent in mid-1975 – at the same time as inflation was rising. 'Stagflation' was born, and Milton Friedman seized the day to move from the periphery of mainstream economics to the centre. This period marked the end of the post-war dominance of economic policy by a consensus that government policy should attempt to keep unemployment low. From then on, the emphasis was on achieving low inflation, and letting the market take care of the level of unemployment.

For a while too, government policy was explicitly Monetarist. In October 1979, following Friedman's dictum that 'Inflation is caused by one thing only – a more rapid increase in the quantity of money than in output' (Friedman 1983, p. 47), and 'The key proposition in monetarism is that the monetary authorities – in the United States, the Federal Reserve System – can control the nominal amount of money expressed in dollars but cannot control the real quantity of money' (Friedman 1983, p. 45), the Federal Reserve under Volcker formally adopted the practice of trying to control the rate of growth of the money supply, rather than controlling the short-term rate of interest.

It was an unhappy experience for all involved, from the Baby Boomers to Milton Friedman himself. Interest rates skyrocketed, with the Federal Reserve rate reaching a peak of over 19 per cent in 1981. Inflation did fall, from a peak of 14¾ per cent in mid-1980, just after the Fed adopted Monetarism, to 2.5 per cent in mid-1983, but this

Figure 2.7. US unemployment and inflation 1960–1990

occurred in the context of a classic deep recession, with unemployment rising from 6 per cent when the Monetarist experiment began, to a post-war peak of 10.8 per cent in 1983.

Milton Friedman was also unhappy, because the money supply was never stabilized as he believed it could and should be: 'monetary growth instead of being steady was highly erratic, indeed far more erratic than it had been earlier'. He blamed this on the Fed not trying hard enough: 'monetarism again has not worked because it has not been carried out' (Friedman 1983, p. 54). The Fed abandoned monetary targeting in mid-1982, and Friedman predicted dire monetary consequences as a result:

> The quantity of money rose at a rate of close to 15 percent from the middle of 1982 to the first quarter of 1983. This raises the distinct possibility that inflation will resume in 1984 or 1985. (Friedman 1983, p. 55)

In fact, nothing of the sort occurred. There was a brief blip in inflation from 2.5 per cent in mid-1983 to 4.8 per cent in mid-1984, but this was in the context of a classic 'Phillips curve' recovery from the Volcker recession; then from mid-1984 till 1987, both unemployment and inflation fell, with the latter reaching a nadir of 1.1 per cent in 1987. Friedman's prediction was spectacularly wrong.[16]

This is not surprising, because so too was his analysis. Key aspects of his argument were consistent with the Neoclassical canon that the money supply was under the control of the Federal Reserve, and that what private banks were doing could be ignored, because they were merely intermediating between savers and borrowers. However, Post Keynesian economists (Moore 1979), some Federal Reserve officials (Holmes 1969), giants of non-mainstream economics (Fisher 1932; Schumpeter 1934), and even some pre-war Neoclassical economists (Pigou 1927), understood that bank lending creates money, and the repayment of bank debt destroys it. This factor, which Friedman and other Neoclassical economists before and since have ignored, was the main cause of the volatility of the money supply that Friedman blamed on the relatively hapless Federal Reserve. As figure 2.8 illustrates, the ups and downs of credit – the annual change in private debt – had and have far more influence on the level of economic activity than the machinations of the Federal Reserve.

2.3 The logic of credit's role in aggregate demand

One of the guiding principles of macroeconomics is that one person's expenditure is another person's income. Thus, if you spend $250 a year at your local pizza shop, the sum of your expenditure on pizza (–$250 from your bank account) and the pizza shop's income from you

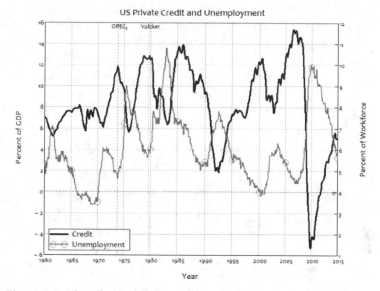

Figure 2.8. The relationship between credit and unemployment

(+$250 into the pizza shop's bank account) is zero. This is because what is an expenditure to you (buying the pizza) is an income to the recipient (selling the pizza). Expenditure and income are two perspectives on precisely the same transaction.

The same principle applies at the macroeconomic level: expenditure IS income. We can use this macroeconomic principle to prove that credit – the change in private debt – adds to both income and expenditure, in a world in which bank lending creates money. This is in contrast to the Neoclassical presumption that, to quote Bernanke, bank loans are 'pure redistributions [that] should have no significant macroeconomic effects' (Bernanke 2000, p. 24). This presumption is true only in a world where banks don't create money, which is the world of Neoclassical textbooks – not the real world.

The proof uses a table that I have christened a *Moore Table*, in honour of the Post Keynesian economist Basil Moore, who pioneered the argument that bank lending creates money (Moore 1979). A Moore Table divides the economy into sectors, and shows expenditure by each sector on every other sector, and the income that results from that expenditure. Each row shows both spending by a given sector – say, Households – and the sectors that receive that expenditure – say, Services and Manufacturing. Expenditure is shown as a negative for the spending sector (since it is a flow of money out of the sector), and a positive for the sectors on which it is spent (since it is a flow of money into the sector). Therefore, each row necessarily sums to zero.

Table 2.2 shows the simplest situation, for a world in which borrowing and lending don't occur. Let's say that Households spend $50 billion a year on Services, and $50 billion a year on Manufacturing; Services spends $30 billion a year on Households and $90 billion on Manufacturing; and Manufacturing spends $70 billion a year on Households and $60 billion on Services. Notice that each row sums to zero, that each column can differ from zero, and that the whole table sums to zero.

We can now classify parts of the table as aggregate expenditure and aggregate income.[17] The negative entries, on the diagonal of the table, are expenditure by each sector, and the negative of this sum is aggregate expenditure. The off-diagonal elements are income received by one sector from another, and the sum of these off-diagonal elements is aggregate income. They are necessarily identical.

Aggregate Expenditure = −(−50−50−30−90−70−60)
Aggregate Expenditure = 350
      Aggregate Income = 50+50+30+90+70+60
      Aggregate Income = 350   (2.1)

The next two tables use symbols rather than numbers, so that $A per year replaces the $50 billion per year spent by Households on Services, $C per year replaces the $30 billion per year spent by Services on Households, and so on.

Table 2.2. A Moore Table showing expenditure IS income for a three-sector economy

	Households	Services	Manufacturing	Sum
Households	**–50–50**	50	50	–50–50+50+50=0
Services	30	**–30–90**	90	30–30–90+90=0
Manufacturing	70	60	**–70–60**	70+60–70–60=0
Sum	–50–50+30+70=0	50–30–90+60=–10	50+90–70–60=+10	0–10+10=0

Expenditure cells highlighted in bold distinguish spending classified as expenditure from spending classified as income.

Table 2.3 covers the model of Loanable Funds, in that Services includes a 'bank' that lends, but does not create money: it takes in new deposits (from other components of the Services sector) and lends them out, as in Neoclassical economic textbooks. The firms whose new savings (also measured in dollars per year) have been lent by the 'Loanable Funds' banks to the other sectors obviously can't spend those savings, so whatever is lent by the Services sector comes at the expense of the Services sector's spending on Households or Manufacturing.[18] For simplicity, let's assume that the reduction in Services' spending is split equally between Households and Manufacturing.

Lending is neither expenditure nor income, so it can't be shown horizontally: instead, it is shown as a transfer across the diagonal, reducing the expenditure of the lender (Services) and increasing the spending of the borrower (Households). Households pays *Interest* dollars per year

Table 2.3. The Moore Table for Loanable Funds

	Households	Services	Manufacturing	Sum
Households	*– (A+B+Credit +Interest)*	*A+Interest*	*B+Credit*	0
Services	*C–Credit/2*	*C–D–Credit*	*D–Credit/2*	0
Manufacturing	*E*	*F*	*– (E+F)*	0
Sum	*(C+E) – (A + B + Credit/2 + Interest)*	*(A+F+Interest) – (C+D–Credit)*	*(B+Credit) + (D–Credit/2) – (E+F)*	0

on its outstanding debt to Services, and since this is both an expenditure and an income, it is shown horizontally.

If you now add up the off-diagonal elements in this table to calculate aggregate income, you will see that *Credit cancels out*: the positive entry for *Credit* as expenditure by Households on Manufacturing is matched by two negative entries of *Credit*/2 for Services' spending on Households and Manufacturing respectively:

$$Aggregate\ Income = (A + Interest) + (B + Credit) + \left(C - \frac{Credit}{2}\right) + \left(D - \frac{Credit}{2}\right) + E + F$$

$$= A + Interest + B + C + D + E + F \qquad (2.2)$$

The only effect of lending on this Loanable Funds model of a monetary economy is that interest payments turn up as part of both expenditure and income. Therefore, if the model of Loanable Funds were an accurate description of what banks do, it *would* be sensible to omit them from macroeconomics as Neoclassical economists do, since, as Bernanke put it, lending and repayment would be 'pure redistributions [which] should have no significant macro-economic effects' (Bernanke 2000, p. 24).

However, we know that Loanable Funds is *not* the real world. On this point, I will be forever grateful to The Bank of England (McLeay et al. 2014a), and the Bundesbank (Deutsche Bundesbank 2017) for enabling me to cite their authority on this matter, rather than having to rely upon the same correct assertions by Post Keynesian economists (Moore 1979; Werner 2014a, 2014b), whom Neoclassical economists have ignored for decades. So, rather than lending being a 'pure redistribution' of existing money, it is a simultaneous creation of new debt and new money. **'Whenever a bank makes a loan, it simultaneously creates a matching deposit in the borrower's bank account, thereby creating new money'**, to quote The Bank of England (McLeay et al. 2014a, p. 14) – including its emphasis. This has been called 'endogenous money' in the Post Keynesian literature to date, but to make it more intelligible to the public, I prefer to call this accurate, real-world description of what banks actually do 'bank-originated money and debt' (with the acronym of BOMD).

It's more complicated to show this than the other tables, since we have to add the banking sector to the table, and we have to include the banking sector's assets – where *Credit* appears as an increase in the banking sector's loans to the Household sector – as well as its liabilities and its equity. Table 2.4 also explicitly shows all spending as passing through the liabilities (deposit accounts) and equity sides of the banking sector's accounts. The Household sector's expenditure on Manufacturing includes *Credit*, as in Loanable Funds, but this credit-financed spending does not come at the expense of any other sector's expenditure: instead, it comes from the creation of new money via the expansion of the banking sector's liabilities and assets.

The key outcome is that *Credit does not cancel out, as it does in Loanable Funds*: there is a single entry for *Credit* in aggregate expenditure – it finances part of the Household sector's purchases from the Manufacturing sector – and a single entry in aggregate income – where it is part of the Manufacturing sector's income:

Aggregate Income =
$$A+(B+Credit)+Interest+C+D+E+F+G+H+I \qquad (2.3)$$

Consequently, in the model shown in table 2.4 – and in the real world – credit is a source of both aggregate demand

Table 2.4. The Moore Table for bank-originated money and debt

	Assets	Liabilities (deposit accounts)			Equity	
	Debt	Households	Services	Manufacturing	Bank	Sum
Households	*Credit*	–(A+B + *Credit* + *Interest*)	A	B + *Credit*	*Interest*	0
Services		C	–(C+D)	D		0
Manufacturing		E	F	–(E+F)		0
Bank		G	H	I	–(G+H+I)	
Sum		(C+E+G) – (A+B + *Credit* + *Interest*)	(A+F+H)– (C+D)	(B+D+I+Credit)– (E+F)	Interest– (G+H+I)	0

and aggregate income. It could only be ignored if it were empirically trivial relative to expenditure and income generated by the turnover of existing money, but this is clearly not the case: credit was as high as 15.3 per cent of US GDP in the fourth quarter of 2006, and as low as −5.1 per cent in the third quarter of 2009. In Spain, the range was even larger: from 34.4 per cent of GDP in Q2-2007 to −19.4 per cent in Q3-2013. Credit is both significant, and far more volatile than the other components of aggregate expenditure.

It is, therefore, *the* explanation for the real-world phenomena of debt-deflationary crises like the Great Recession, the Great Depression and the Panic of 1837. Neoclassical economics, by ignoring banks, debt and money in its macroeconomic models, is ignoring the main factors that drive economic performance and also cause economic crises.

2.4 Negative credit, economic crises and economic policy

Neoclassical economists appropriated Nassim Taleb's phrase 'The Black Swan' (Taleb 2010) to assert that the Great Recession was impossible to predict, because crises like it are so rare, and because their causes are fundamentally random. Called 'exogenous shocks' by Neoclassicals, random events are the only factors that cause Neoclassical models of the economy to deviate from equilibrium. Therefore, 'exogenous shocks' must have caused the Great Recession. The Boston College Economics Professor Peter Ireland put it this way:

> In terms of its macroeconomics, was the Great Recession of 2007–09 really that different from what came before? The results derived here from estimating and simulating a New Keynesian model provide the answer: partly yes and partly no.

These results suggest that largely, *the pattern of exogenous demand and supply disturbances* that caused the Great Moderation to end and the Great Recession to begin was quite similar to the patterns generating each of the two previous downturns in 1990–91 and 2001. Compared to those from previous episodes, however, *the series of adverse shocks* hitting the US economy most recently *lasted longer and became more intense, contributing both to the exceptional length and severity of the Great Recession.* (Ireland 2011, p. 51, emphasis added)

The policy prescription from this analysis is to do ... nothing at all, beyond the Boy Scout motto of 'be prepared'. *From the perspective of the Neoclassical paradigm*, crises like the Great Recession can't be anticipated, let alone made less likely by economic policy. We can only deal with their consequences after they happen.

This is akin to Aristotle's theory of comets (which was preserved in Ptolemaic astronomy) that comets were unpredictable, because they were atmospheric phenomena (Aristotle 350 BCE [1952], Part 7). The Copernican scientific revolution, which overthrew this worldview, showed that comets were inherently predictable, as they are celestial objects orbiting the Sun.[19]

Similarly, the 'unpredictability' of crises like the Great Recession is a product of the Neoclassical paradigm's false Loanable Funds model of money. The correct BODM model shows that crises are caused by credit turning negative (Vague 2019), and that most recessions are caused by credit declining, but not quite going negative. This causal relationship between credit (which is identical in magnitude to the annual change in private debt) and economic performance endows capitalist economies with a tendency to accumulate higher and higher levels of private debt. This phenomenon is most evident in that most capitalist of economies, the United States of America (see figure 2.9).

Figure 2.9 identifies America's three great economic crises: the Great Recession, the Great Depression, and the

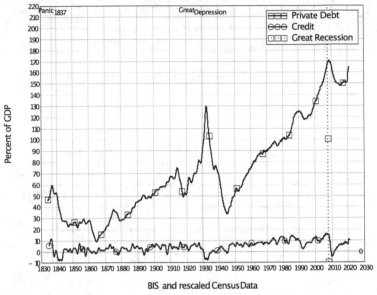

Figure 2.9. Private debt and credit in the USA since 1834

'Panic of 1837'. What, you haven't heard of the 'Panic of 1837'? Neither had I before I produced this chart, using historical Census data (Census Bureau 1949, 1975).[20] After I did, I knew there had to have been a crisis then, and found that the 'Panic of 1837' was described at the time as 'an economic crisis so extreme as to erase all memories of previous financial disorders' (Roberts 2012, p. 24).

In each of these crises, credit plunged from a historically high level, turned negative, and remained negative for a substantial period (see table 2.5). Each crisis turned around only when the decline of credit stopped. But the renewed growth engendered by rising credit came at the expense of a rising private debt-to-GDP ratio, with this rise terminated either by another crisis, or by wars that drove the private debt ratio down dramatically because of the 'war economy' boost to GDP: nominal GDP growth reached 32 per cent p.a. during the US Civil War in 1861–5, 29 per cent during the First World War (1914–18), and 29

Table 2.5. Magnitude of credit and duration of negative credit in the USA's major economic crises

	Credit (annual change in private debt)			
	Credit as percent of GDP			Years
Crisis	Maximum	Minimum	Change	Negative duration[a]
Panic of 1837	12.2	–8.9	21.1	6.2
Great Depression	9.1	–9.1	18.2	8.2
Great Recession	15.4	–5.3	20.7	2.6

[a] This is measured from the first negative month to the last, but includes some periods of positive credit (most of 1839, and late 1935 till late 1936).

per cent again during the Second World War (1939–45), far exceeding the maximum growth rate of credit during those periods (0.2 per cent of GDP p.a., 8.6 per cent and 4.5 per cent, respectively).

This is no way to run an economy, but it is what we are stuck with while economic policy is dominated by a theory of economics that ignores banks, private debt, money and credit. However, with a new, monetary paradigm, several things become evident: we should stop the level of private debt from getting too high, and credit-based demand should not be allowed to become too large a component of aggregate demand (Bezemer and Grydaki 2014).

2.5 An integrated view of deficits and credit

One striking feature of figure 2.6 is the rarity of government surpluses, despite the never-ending political rhetoric about achieving them. The only period of sustained surpluses was the 1920s, when the government maintained a surplus of roughly 1 per cent of GDP each year. The 'Roaring Twenties', as the decade became known, was a time of great economic prosperity, and in his 1928 State of the

Union Address, President Calvin Coolidge attributed this success to the government surplus:

> No Congress of the United States ever assembled, on surveying the state of the Union, has met with a more pleasing prospect than that which appears at the present time ... a surplus has been produced. One-third of the national debt has been paid ... the national income has increased nearly 50 per cent ... That is constructive economy in the highest degree. It is the corner stone of prosperity. It should not fail to be continued. (Coolidge 1928)

In fact, the surplus was depressing the economy, by taking the equivalent of just under 1 per cent of GDP out of private bank accounts every year. At the same time, the private sector was borrowing on average 5 per cent of GDP every year, and using this to gamble on financial assets in an orgy of debt-fuelled speculation, initially in a forgotten but significant housing bubble (Vague 2019), and then in the stock market.

As Coolidge lauded himself for causing government debt to fall from 30 per cent to 15 per cent of GDP, private debt rose from 55 per cent to 100 per cent of GDP. All was good as the private debt level rose, because as explained earlier, positive credit adds to aggregate demand (for speculative assets as well as goods and services, though the former doesn't turn up in GDP). But when debt stopped rising, credit turned negative, and aggregate demand collapsed, as did the stock market. Far from being 'the corner stone of prosperity', Coolidge's surpluses helped pave the road to the Great Depression.

We can avoid Coolidge's mistake of attributing all of the economy's performance during the 1920s to the government surplus by building a simple *Minsky* model that integrates government money creation via deficit spending, and bank money creation via credit – see figure 2.10. In this simplified model, government spending and taxation is summarized by a deficit, and private bank

Banking Sector

Flows ↓ / Stock Vars →	Asset			Liability		Equity	A-L-E
	Reserves▼	$Bonds_B$▼	$Loans_F$▼	Firms ▼	Workers▼	$Banks_E$	0
Initial Conditions	0	150	280	250	30	150	0
Government Deficit	Deficit			Deficit			0
Buy or Sell Bonds	-Bonds	Bonds					0
Pay Interest on Bonds	$Interest_B$					$Interest_B$	0
Bank Lending			Credit	Credit			0
Pay Interest on Loans				-Interest		Interest	0
Hire Workers				-Wages	Wages		0
Bank spending				$Cons_B$		$-Cons_B$	0
Worker consumption				$Cons_W$	$-Cons_W$		0

Figure 2.10. The banking sector's view of a mixed fiat-credit economy. See http://www.profstevekeen.com/minsky/

money creation is summarized by credit, both of which can be either positive or negative.

One general point this model illustrates is worth mentioning: for an operation to create or destroy money in a modern banking system, one of its two entries must occur on the asset side of the private banking system's ledger, and the other must occur on the liabilities side. Government deficits, private bank credit, and Treasury Bond sales to the public, all qualify; Treasury sales of bonds to private banks, and central bank purchases of bonds from private banks, do not.

The simulation shown in figure 2.11 is a counterfactual to Coolidge's laudatory portrayal of his surplus. It marries the same surplus – 1 per cent of GDP per year – to a private sector also trying to achieve the same aim – to pay its debt to the banking sector down by 1 per cent of GDP per year. The result, after a transient period of growth as the model settles down from its initial conditions, is a declining GDP. With both the government and non-bank public trying to reduce indebtedness, both are instead reducing the money supply. With money turning over more than once per year, GDP falls faster than debt falls, and 'Fisher's Paradox' asserts itself as the private debt-to-GDP ratio starts to rise:

> liquidation defeats itself. While it diminishes the number of dollars owed, ... it increases the value of each dollar owed. Then, *the very effort of individuals to lessen their*

burden of debts increases it, because of the mass effect of the stampede to liquidate in swelling each dollar owed. Then we have the great paradox which, I submit, is the chief secret of most, if not all, great depressions: *The more the debtors pay, the more they owe.* (Fisher 1933, p. 344)

Fisher himself acquired this wisdom the hard way. He was his day's Paul Krugman: a famous mainstream economist (and also inventor) who also wrote a column for the *New York Times*. He took the profits from his inventions and levered them into the stock market with margin debt, which in the 1920s allowed a speculator to put down a deposit of $1,000 and borrow $9,000, to buy $10,000 worth of shares with a $10,000 'margin account'.[21]

The borrower paid interest on the loan of course, but the leverage meant that, if markets rose 10 per cent, then before expenses, the speculator doubled his money: $10,000 worth of shares became $11,000, doubling the speculator's net worth from $1,000 to $2,000. But there was a catch: if the market fell 10 per cent, then the speculator had to top up the account to keep it at $10,000. This would wipe the speculator's equity out – from $1,000 to zero (before expenses). If the speculator couldn't comply

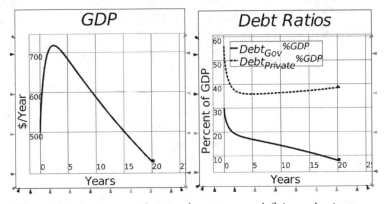

Figure 2.11. An integrated view of government deficits and private sector credit. See http://www.profstevekeen.com/minsky/

with his ready cash, then the stockbroker was entitled by the margin contract to liquidate *any* of the speculator's assets: it was an unlimited liability. Most speculators were confident that this would never happen, and for most of the decade, they were right: while the margin debt-to-GDP ratio increased 5.5 times between the stock market's all-time low point in 1921 and October 1929, the stock market itself rose sixfold.[22] Then the stock market jitters began, which Fisher downplayed. On 16 October 1929, he was quoted in the *Times* as saying at a conference that 'Stock prices have reached what looks like a permanently high plateau.' He continued:

> I do not feel that there will soon, if ever, be a fifty or sixty point break below present levels, such as Mr. Babson has predicted. *I expect to see the stock market a good deal higher than it is today within a few months.* (Fisher 1929, p. 8, emphasis added)

Just two weeks later, the Dow Jones Industrial Average plunged over 60 points in two days, losing more than 20 per cent of its value. Margin calls wiped out levered speculators like Fisher immediately, and took the economy down with it, because margin debt had exploded from a mere 1 per cent of GDP in the early 1920s to 13 per cent in October 1929 (see figure 2.12). This is why the Twenties roared – and largely also why the Thirties wailed.

The collapse of margin debt from over 13 per cent to under 1 per cent of GDP in the first two years of the 1930s was the chief reason that the Stock Market Crash of 1929 was so deadly, compared to subsequent crashes in 1987, 2000 and 2007, and why it ushered in the Great Depression, which itself did much to cause the rise of fascism and the Second World War.

As awful as those crises were, they had one strong positive economic side-effect, from which the next generation – the Baby Boomers – benefited handsomely. The combination of massive government spending and

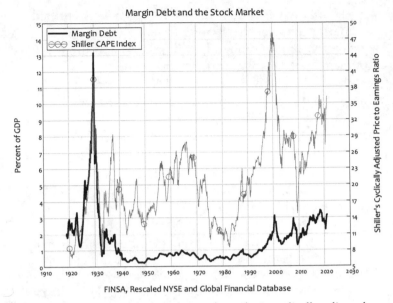

Figure 2.12. Margin debt and the stock market's cyclically-adjusted price-to-earnings ratio (CAPE) since 1910

constrained private sector consumption during the Second World War enabled the deleveraging that commenced in 1933 to continue. By the end of the war, private debt had fallen to 33 per cent of GDP, from its deflation-driven peak of 130 per cent in 1932 (see figure 2.9). This low level of private debt, along with the substantial level of fiat-based money created during the Second World War, low interest rates and regular government deficits, meant that the financial burden on the private sector in the 1950s and 1960s was trivial. It was as if the slate had been wiped clean by a classical debt jubilee.

Not realizing any of this, and certainly not understanding the incredible reluctance of their parents and grandparents to go into debt, after the tribulations of the 1970s and early 1980s, the Baby Boomers restarted the borrowing bubble, culminating in the telecommunications, dotcom and finally subprime bubbles, which drove private debt to its highest level in US history (and in most of the rest of the developed world). After this crisis, with Neoclassical economists of the Baby Boomer generation in charge of government policy, private debt fell by only 20 per cent from its Great Recession peak of 170 per cent of GDP. Even before Covid-19, it was well above the previous peak in 1932. We need to reduce private debt back to its levels during that Golden Age – but we should find a better way of doing so than another world war.

2.6 A Modern Debt Jubilee

The monetary perspective developed in the previous sections shows that the real-world roles of private and public debt, and of credit and government deficits, are the exact opposite of what the Neoclassical conventional wisdom asserts. Private debt, not government debt, is the primary cause of economic crises (Bezemer and Grydaki 2014; Jordà et al. 2011; Keen 2020b; Vague 2019; Zhang and Bezemer 2014). Credit, and not government deficits, is dangerous when it is large relative to GDP. Rising private debt, not rising government debt, is the main indicator of an approaching crisis. Private debt, not government debt, can depress economic activity because it is too high. These insights indicate that the levels of private debt and credit are economic indicators of at least as much importance as the customary ones of the unemployment rate and the inflation rate. They should be monitored as closely, and economic policy should aim to keep them both relatively low.

But that leaves the issue of what to do when Neoclassical economics, by not only ignoring private debt, but also by actively arguing in favour of debt financing of business instead of equity financing (Modigliani and Merton 1958; Wigglesworth 2020), has helped drive private debt to at least three times its Golden Age level. If capitalism is ever to have another Golden Age, then we need to reduce the private debt-to-GDP ratio by at least as much as it was reduced during the 1930s and 1940s. This could be done in exactly the same way that the government runs a deficit today, in a way that does not advantage those who gambled with borrowed money over those that did not, and without causing inflation – and even, if it is so desired, without increasing aggregate demand – by what I call a *Modern Debt Jubilee*.

Figure 2.13 shows the basic accounting logic of a Modern Debt Jubilee (Coppola 2019; Hudson 2018). Firstly, the Treasury issues every adult resident, debtor and saver alike, the same sum of fiat-based money. If this amount were $100,000 per American over 15 years old, the total in 2021 would be $24 trillion – 70 per cent of the level of pre-Covid private sector debt, and roughly 110 per cent of GDP. Those who had bank debt would be required to reduce it by that amount. Those who were debt free, or whose debts were less than $100,000, would be required to buy newly-issued corporate shares, the revenue from which would have to be used to cancel corporate debt, and replace it with equity.

The banks would not lose out in this process. Instead, their reserves would rise by precisely as much as their debt-based assets would fall. Then, they would use these excess reserves to buy Jubilee Bonds, the interest on which would generate an income stream for banks, in partial compensation for the loss of income from interest on household and corporate debt.

No additional money, or spending power, would be created directly. Instead, there would be an increase in fiat-backed money, and an equivalent decline in credit-backed money. For corporations, shareholder equity would rise, and corporate debt would fall. Private debt would go from 150 per cent of GDP (pre-Covid-19) to 40 per cent of GDP – roughly the level it was at the start of the Golden Age of Capitalism.

This would also reduce the obscene increase in inequality that has been the direct and deliberate result of the

Private Banks

Flows ↓ / Stock Vars →	Reserves▼	Bonds▼	Loans$_D$▼	Loans$_F$▼	Debtors▼	Savers▼	Firms▼	Loans$_{CB}^{PB}$▼	Banks$_E$	A-L-E
Initial Conditions	100	0	400	600	100	400	400	100	100	0
Jubilee for Debtors	Jubilee$_D$				Jubilee$_D$					0
Jubilee for Savers	Jubilee$_S$					Jubilee$_S$				0
Debtors pay off Debt			-Jubilee$_R$		-Jubilee$_R$					0
Savers buy shares						-Jubilee$_I$	Jubilee$_I$			0
Firms pay off Debt				-Jubilee$_F$			-Jubilee$_F$			0
Treasury sells Jubilee Bonds	-Jubilee$_B$	Jubilee$_B$								0
Interest on Jubilee Bonds	Interest$_I$								Interest$_I$	0

Savers

Flows ↓ / Stock Vars →	Savers▼	Shares$_I$▼		Savers$_E$	A-L-E
Initial Conditions	400	0		400	0
Savers buy shares	-Jubilee$_I$	Jubilee$_I$			0
Jubilee for Savers	Jubilee$_S$			Jubilee$_S$	0

Debtors

Flows ↓ / Stock Vars →	Debtors▼	Loans$_D$▼	Debtors$_E$	A-L-E
Initial Conditions	100	400	-300	0
Jubilee for Debtors	Jubilee$_D$		Jubilee$_D$	0
Debtors pay off Debt	-Jubilee$_R$	-Jubilee$_R$		0

Firms

Flows ↓ / Stock Vars →	Firms▼	Loans$_F$▼	Shares$_I$▼	Firms$_E$	A-L-E
Initial Conditions	400	600	0	-200	0
Firms pay off Debt	-Jubilee$_F$	-Jubilee$_F$			0
Savers buy shares	Jubilee$_I$		Jubilee$_I$		0

Central Bank

Flows ↓ / Stock Vars →	Loans$_{CB}^{PB}$▼	Reserves▼	Treasury▼	CB$_E$	A-L-E
Initial Conditions	100	100	0	0	0
Interest on Jubilee Bonds		Interest$_I$	-Interest$_I$		0
Treasury sells Jubilee Bonds		-Jubilee$_D$	Jubilee$_B$		0
Jubilee for Debtors		Jubilee$_D$	-Jubilee$_D$		0
Jubilee for Savers		Jubilee$_S$	-Jubilee$_S$		0

Treasury

Flows ↓ / Stock Vars →	Treasury▼	Bonds▼	Treasury$_E$	A-L-E
Initial Conditions	0	0	0	0
Interest on Jubilee Bonds	-Interest$_I$		-Interest$_I$	0
Treasury sells Jubilee Bonds	Jubilee$_B$	Jubilee$_B$		0
Jubilee for Debtors	-Jubilee$_D$		-Jubilee$_D$	0
Jubilee for Savers	-Jubilee$_S$		-Jubilee$_S$	0

Figure 2.13. Accounting for a Modern Debt Jubilee. See http://www.profstevekeen.com/minsky/

program of 'Quantitative Easing' (QE) that the Federal Reserve has followed since 2010. As Bernanke himself put it in an OpEd for *The Washington Post*, 'higher stock prices will boost consumer wealth and help increase confidence, which can also spur spending. Increased spending will lead to higher incomes and profits that, in a virtuous circle, will further support economic expansion' (Bernanke 2010). QE, which initially saw the Fed promise to be a net buyer of bonds from banks to the tune of $80 billion per month, or almost $1 trillion per year, encouraged financial corporations to buy shares in place of the bonds they had sold to the Fed.

QE was the major factor in the rise of the S&P500 from its nadir of 666 in early 2009 to almost six times as much in 2020. This boosted wealth dramatically – but only the wealth of those who owned shares. The vast majority of the population own no shares directly, and only a trivial fraction of the stock market's overall valuation via pension schemes and the like. This policy decision, made by and undertaken by the Neoclassical economists who run the Federal Reserve, amplified the inequality already created by the preceding debt-financed bubbles – a point I'll elaborate upon in the next chapter. It is a policy mistake that should be reversed, and a Modern Debt Jubilee could do it.

You will, I hope, already know that QE didn't involve any taxes. It was entirely a Federal Reserve action, because the increase in the Fed's liabilities – the huge rise in the reserves of private banks – was matched by an equivalent increase in the Fed's assets, its holdings of both government and corporate bonds. Unlike QE, a Modern Debt Jubilee would necessarily involve the Treasury, as shown in figure 2.13, and the negative equity generated for the Treasury would be identical to the positive equity created for savers and debtors (and the banking system, via interest payments on Jubilee Bonds).

A Modern Debt Jubilee could thus help us escape the debt trap that Neoclassical economics has led us into. The next step is to stop that trap from recurring, by taming the 'roving cavaliers of credit'.

2.7 Taming 'the roving cavaliers of credit'

Some of Marx's greatest and truest rhetorical flourishes occurred in Chapter 33 of Volume III of *Capital* (Marx 1894, Chapter 33), when he discussed the financial system:

> A high rate of interest can also indicate, as it did in 1857, that the country is undermined by *the roving cavaliers of*

credit who can afford to pay a high interest because they pay it out of other people's pockets (whereby, however, they help to determine the rate of interest for all), and *meanwhile they live in grand style on anticipated profits.* Simultaneously, precisely this can incidentally provide a very profitable business for manufacturers and others. *Returns become wholly deceptive as a result of the loan system …*

Talk about centralisation! The credit system, which has its focus in the so-called national banks and the big money-lenders and usurers surrounding them, constitutes enormous centralisation, and gives this class of parasites the fabulous power, not only to periodically despoil industrial capitalists, but also to *interfere in actual production in a most dangerous manner – and this gang knows nothing about production and has nothing to do with it.* (Marx 1894, Chapter 33, emphasis added)

Marx's disparaging outsider's remarks about bankers are confirmed by insider accounts today, including that of ex-banker and philanthropist Richard Vague, whose *A Brief History of Doom* (Vague 2019) is a magisterial account of the role of bankers, credit and debt in causing all of the world's major economic crises before Covid-19.[23]

Vague acknowledges, as I do, the creative role that credit can play in a capitalist economy:

Take away private debt, and commerce as we know it would slow to a crawl. The world suffered crisis after crisis in the 1800s, but per-capita-GDP increased thirtyfold in that century, and private debt was integral to that growth. Many of those nineteenth-century crises were rooted in the overexpansion of railroads, but they left behind an impressively extensive network of rails from which countries still benefit. (Vague 2019, p. 16)

But he echoes Marx from insider knowledge about the incentives for irresponsible over-lending that are rife in banks:

... financial crises recur so frequently ... that we have to wonder why lending booms happen at all. The answer is this: growth in lending is what brings lenders higher compensation, advancement, and recognition. Until a crisis point is reached, rapid lending growth can bring euphoria and staggering wealth ... Lending booms are driven by competition, inevitably accompanied by the fear of falling behind or missing out ...

Having spent a lifetime in the industry, I can report that there is almost always the desire to grow loans aggressively and increase wealth ... So the better and more profound question is, why are there periods in which loan growth isn't booming? ... when lenders are chastened – often in the years following a crisis. (Vague 2019, pp. 7–8)

While financial instability cannot be wholly eliminated from capitalism – for reasons that will become evident in the next chapter – the most egregious elements of irresponsible bank lending can be addressed by limitations on what banks are allowed to lend for. These limitations should be part and parcel of being granted the privilege and power to create money that comes with a banking licence, especially since history provides ample evidence that, without controls, this privilege will be abused. They should constrain or eliminate lending that finances asset price bubbles, and direct lending as much as is possible towards investment and essential consumption rather than speculation.

Once the role of credit in aggregate demand is understood, it's easy to extend this to asset markets, in which credit plays a major role. With mortgage debt as the main means by which houses are purchased, there is a causal relationship between new mortgages – or mortgage credit – and the house price level. There is, therefore, a link between change in mortgage credit and change in house prices (Zhang and Bezemer 2014). The same logic applies to change in margin credit and change in stock prices. The correlation between change in mortgage credit and change in house prices since 1971 is 0.64, while the correlation

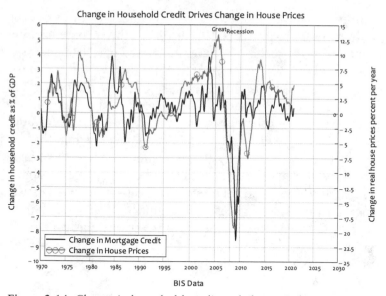

Figure 2.14. Change in household credit and change in house prices (correlation 0.64)

between change in margin credit and change in Shiller's CAPE index since 1990 – when margin debt began to rise again after fifty years of being below 0.5 per cent of GDP – is also 0.64 (see figure 2.14).

This type of borrowing drives asset price bubbles, and does precious little to benefit society. We need means by which this kind of borrowing can be discouraged, while lending for productive purposes can be enhanced.

2.7.1 'The pill'

At present, if two individuals with the same savings and income are competing for a property, then the one who can secure a larger loan wins. This reality gives borrowers an incentive to want to have the loan-to-valuation ratio increased, which underpins the finance sector's ability to expand debt for property purchases.

I instead propose basing the maximum debt that can be used to purchase a property on the income (actual or imputed) of the property itself. Lenders would only be able to lend up to a fixed multiple of the income-earning capacity of the property being purchased – regardless of the income of the borrower. A useful multiple would be 10, so that if a property rented for $30,000 p.a., the maximum amount of money that could be borrowed by anyone to purchase it, regardless of their income, would be $300,000.

Under this regime, if two parties were vying for the same property, the one that raised more money via savings would win. There would therefore be a negative feedback relationship between leverage and house prices: a general increase in house prices would mean a general fall in leverage. This would also encourage treating housing as it should be treated: a long-lived consumer good, rather than an object of speculation.

2.7.2 Jubilee shares

The key factor that allows Ponzi schemes to work in asset markets is the 'Greater Fool' promise that a share bought today for $1 can be sold tomorrow for $10. No interest rate, no regulation, can hold against the charge to insanity that such a feasible prospect foments. The vast majority of activity on the stock market is also the sale of existing shares by one speculator to another, which raises no capital for the company in question. The primary market – the sale of new shares by a company to raise capital – is trivial by comparison.

I propose the redefinition of shares in such a way that the enticement of limitless price appreciation can be removed, and the primary market can take precedence over the secondary market. A share bought in an IPO (initial public offering) or rights offer would last forever (for as long as the company exists) as now, with all the rights it currently confers. It could be sold into the secondary market with all the same privileges. But on a subsequent sale, say the fifth, it would have a life span of fifty years, at which point it would terminate.

The objective of this proposal is to eliminate the appeal of using debt to buy existing shares, while still making it attractive to fund innovative firms or start-ups via the primary market, and still making purchase of the share of an established company on the secondary market attractive to those seeking an annuity income.

This basic proposal might be refined, while still maintaining the primary objective of making leveraged speculation on the price of existing shares unappealing. The termination date could be made a function of how long a share was held; the number of sales on the secondary market before the Jubilee effect applied could be altered. But the basic idea must be to make borrowing money to gamble on the prices of existing shares a very unattractive proposition.

2.7.3 Entrepreneurial equity loans

Entrepreneurs, in Schumpeter's compelling vision of their role in capitalism's development (Schumpeter 1934), are people with a good idea but no money with which to turn these ideas into products. Today, credit to entrepreneurs from banks is almost non-existent, and for good reason: most entrepreneurs will fail, and banks that lend to them lose their capital, while only securing an interest-rate return from those entrepreneurs who succeed.

One way to encourage banks to lend to entrepreneurs in return for equity, rather than debt, is via 'entrepreneurial equity loans' (EELs). Banks would still lose money on those entrepreneurs that failed, but could make a capital gain as well as a flow of dividends on those entrepreneurs who succeeded.[24]

2.8 Shifting the monetary paradigm

I am often asked what I would keep of Neoclassical economics in a new paradigm. My answer is that I would keep as much of Neoclassical economics as modern astronomy kept of Ptolemaic astronomy – which is to say, nothing at all.

On its own, that answer may seem both arrogant and flippant: surely there is something of value in all the work done by Neoclassical economists? Yes, there are skerricks of merit in the entire edifice. But I hope that it is evident after this chapter on money that nothing of worth remains of the Neoclassical perspective on money and banking, once the reality that banks create money is accepted. Rather than being irrelevant to macro-economics, banks, private debt and money are essential. Rather than playing no role in macroeconomics, credit is a significant component of aggregate demand and income, and, given its volatility, it is the 'causa causans' (Keynes 1937, p. 221) that drives macroeconomics. Financial crises, rather than being 'Black Swans', are products of credit turning negative. Private debt, not government debt, is dangerous when it is high relative to GDP. Governments should normally run deficits to create identical surpluses for the non-government sectors. Government debt does not burden future generations but instead generates monetary assets for current ones.

All the Neoclassical arguments about money are invalid: there is nothing left to keep. The same applies to the next, more technical failing of Neoclassical economics: its obsession with modelling the economy as if it has a stable equilibrium.

3

Our complex world

Three of the most complex systems we know about are the human brain, which enables you to read this book, the economy, which is its subject, and the biosphere, in which both our brains and our economy evolved.

These systems are called *complex*, not because they are complicated – though of course, they are – but because they interact – both within themselves, and with each other – in complex ways. Neither our present, nor our past, let alone our future, can be understood without acknowledging the feedbacks that exist both between each of these systems, and within them.

Today, the interactions between these systems have reached a fever-pitch. Covid-19 has reminded us that we are part of the biosphere, rather than separate from and above it. It laid waste to our economies, but the form and magnitude of its damage were altered by how we, as a civilization, reacted to it. In September 2020, it coincided with dramatic fires in much of the western United States, and serious floods in the south due to a historically high number of hurricanes. This coincidence made both problems worse, because minimizing the spread of Covid-19 required isolating people, while saving them from wildfires and floods required evacuating them *en masse*, and housing them together in emergency facilities. One crisis compounded the other.

Economics has attempted to deal with feedback effects via the concept of equilibrium. The state of equilibrium is one in which the system's key variables are not changing. However, economists – even some non-Neoclassical ones – claim that this state of rest 'does not "ignore" time', but rather 'allows enough time for changes ... to have their *full* effects' (Steedman 1992, p. 146). Effectively, conventional economic theory has taken the shortcut of working in terms of the equilibrium of the economic system, rather than worrying about what it regards as the transient dynamics of the approach to equilibrium. It assumes, in other words, that any cyclical process will ultimately achieve a state of rest: feedbacks are presumed to dampen oscillations over time.

A century ago, the mathematician Alfred Lotka proved that this presumption is false, when he considered the dynamics of interacting species – a predator species and its prey. In his example, the 'prey' was grass, and the 'predators' were cows. Starting with a small number of cows in a paddock, the amount of grass will grow, because there aren't enough cows to eat all the new grass. But this provides ideal conditions for cows to breed, so the number of cows will rise. A larger number of cows will ultimately consume grass at a faster rate than it grows, causing the paddock to start to turn bare. As this starts to happen, there isn't enough feed for all the cows to survive, so some die of starvation, leading back to where we started with a small number of cows. Figure 3.1 shows this as a cyclical process.

Lotka expected that this would lead to diminishing cycles over time, so that the number of cows and the amount of grass would ultimately converge to equilibrium values. Instead, he found, to his surprise, that the quantity of both grass and cows would oscillate indefinitely:

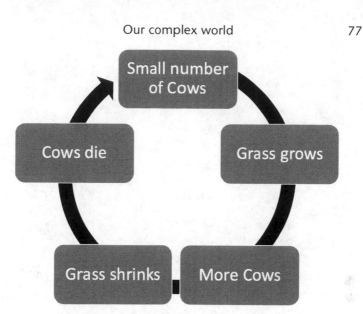

Figure 3.1. The cyclical interaction of grass and cows

> It was, therefore, with considerable surprise that the writer, on applying his method to certain special cases, found these to lead to undamped, and hence indefinitely continued, oscillations. (Lotka 1920, p. 410)

Lotka's discovery was the conception of what is today known as *complex systems* analysis. An essential aspect of this approach is that you *cannot* do what conventional economists do: you cannot use equilibrium as a short-cut. For most complex systems, the equilibrium tells you not where the system will ultimately end up, but *where the system will never be*. Rather than converging to an equilibrium, complex systems tend to oscillate indefinitely – as Lotka found in his model of cows and grass.

The dynamics of a 'predator-prey' model, as Lotka's discovery was called, are shown in figure 3.2, using the example of sharks and fish, rather than cows and grass. The model has an equilibrium,[1] shown by the lines in the time plots and the dot in the phase plot, but it is 'neutral': if the model starts out of equilibrium, it will never converge to it, but neither will it move further away.

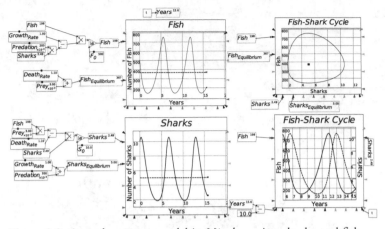

Figure 3.2. A predator-prey model in *Minsky*, using sharks and fish. See http://www.profstevekeen.com/minsky/

One limitation of Lotka's model was that the oscillations were always of the same size and frequency, which is not what we observe in the real world. Cycles in real-world systems like the economy are *aperiodic*: there are booms and busts, but the amplitude and frequency of every boom and bust is different to those that have gone before. Most of the very few economists who knew of Lotka's discovery ignored it for this reason. Instead, the explanation of cycles that became dominant in economics was that they were the result of external ('exogenous') shocks disturbing an otherwise stable system. Ragnar Frisch, the founding editor of the journal *Econometrica*, put it this way a decade after Lotka:

> The majority of the economic oscillations which we encounter seem to be explained most plausibly as free oscillations. In many cases they seem to be produced by the fact that certain exterior impulses hit the economic mechanism and thereby initiate more or less regular oscillations ...
>
> [T]he source of energy which maintains the economic cycles are erratic shocks ... New innovations and exploitations do not come regularly ... these irregular jerks may cause more or less regular cyclical movements ... 'If you

hit a wooden rocking-horse with a club, the movement of the horse will be very different to that of the club.' (Frisch 1933, pp. 1, 28)

This rejection by economists of the complex systems argument that cycles are endogenous – caused by dynamics within the economy itself, rather than from shocks coming from outside the economy – was shown to be invalid three decades later, by the discovery of what was called, for a while, 'chaotic dynamics' in weather systems. The discovery was first revealed in a paper with the telling title of 'Deterministic Nonperiodic Flow' (Lorenz 1963).

At the time, meteorologists used linear models to try to predict the weather. Edward Lorenz was dissatisfied with this, because one aspect of the weather – for example, air temperature – influenced other aspects – such as wind speed – *nonlinearly*. Changes in temperature would multiply wind strength, and not merely add to it. To illustrate this, he took an extremely complicated model of fluid dynamics and reduced it to a simple model with just three variables (x, y and z) and three constants (a, b and c).

Superficially, this is only slightly more complicated than Lotka's model, which has two variables and four constants. But the behaviour was totally different: the model generated cycles which varied in both amplitude and frequency, in a way that appeared chaotic at first – but then Lorenz discovered that, beneath the apparently 'chaotic' movements of the variables x, y and z over time, lay the beautiful pattern of x or y plotted against z that he dubbed the 'Butterfly Effect' (see figure 3.3).

Lorenz's paper introduced the world to a whole new type of equilibrium: the 'strange attractor'. This is an equilibrium, which the system will approach from some distance away, but from which it is repelled when it gets closer. There are two strange attractors in Lorenz's model, located in the vacant spaces within the two butterfly wings. There are three equilibria in the model, *all* of which are unstable for realistic parameter values.

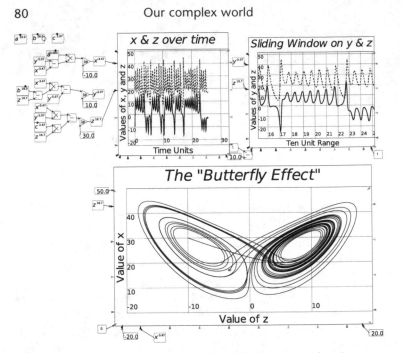

Figure 3.3. Lorenz's model of aperiodic cycles in the weather. See
http://www.profstevekeen.com/minsky/

The essential feature causing this behaviour is the
interaction of three or more system variables in nonlinear
ways. Both Lotka's and Lorenz's models have nonlinear
terms – terms where one variable is multiplied by another.
Lotka's model generated periodic cycles of fixed magnitude
because he only had two species in it – though more can
easily be added. Lorenz's model, with three variables, was
the minimum number needed to generate aperiodic cycles,
like those we see in the real world (Li and Yorke 1975).

The reason why a dynamic system with three variables
is so different to one with two comes down to geometry:
one of the rules of differential equations is that, if you
plot the values of a system's variables against each other
in any one simulation, the paths can't intersect. With two
variables, the pattern of one variable against another gives
you a two-dimensional shape, like something you can

draw on a tabletop, without ever lifting your finger off the table, and without ever crossing your path.

This leaves you with just five options: to spiral in, ultimately reaching a point; to spiral out, ultimately running out of table; to spiral in, converging on a curve (like a circle) but never actually getting there; to spiral out, also converging on a circle; or to stay on a closed path forever – precisely repeating the same pattern, rather than intersecting it.[2]

With three variables, you get a three-dimensional shape – like a box. Now repeat the same process in an imaginary box above your table. You can easily draw complicated shapes, like Lorenz's butterfly, without ever intersecting your path.

Lorenz's discovery transformed meteorology: one of the main reasons that weather forecasts today are so much more accurate than they were half a century ago – even with climate change destabilizing the weather – is because meteorologists took Lorenz's advice and built large-scale, *nonlinear* models of the atmosphere. His discovery strongly influenced most other physical sciences as well.

But economics, as a notoriously insular social science (Leijonhufvud 1973), largely ignored Lorenz. Though a handful of economists, myself included, took Lorenz's results to heart, the vast majority continued with Frisch's approach of treating the economy as a stable system, whose fluctuations are caused by 'exogenous shocks'.

So complex systems models can explain aperiodic cycles in a system. Why, apart from ignorance, do economists not analyse the economy as a complex system, and continue to use Frisch's invalid framework of a stable system subject to exogenous shocks?

The one defence that could be made is just that: that the economy is 'too complex' to model it either out of equilibrium, or with fundamentally nonlinear components. There are many things that are much simpler to do when you assume that you can ignore nonlinear interactions in a system. For a start, a nonlinear system with three or more variables cannot, in general, be solved analytically. Linear models, on the other hand, in general can be solved. It is also much easier to estimate a linear model and fit it to data than a nonlinear one. Linear models, even ones with lots of equations, are inherently simpler than nonlinear models, even small ones, and the urge to 'keep it simple' runs deep in all sciences.

But as Einstein was once paraphrased, the idea is to keep things 'as simple as possible, *but no simpler*'. Einstein's actual statement was that:

> It can scarcely be denied that the supreme goal of all theory is to make the irreducible basic elements as simple and as few as possible *without having to surrender the adequate representation of a single datum of experience.* (Einstein 1934, p. 165, emphasis added)

The best illustration that the very complicated, but fundamentally linear, stable-equilibrium models that mainstream economists prefer violate this principle is their failure to anticipate the Global Financial Crisis of 2007–10. In fact, as noted earlier (Cotis 2007, p. 7), 2008 was going to be a fabulous year, according to these models. The predictions of the OECD's 'Dynamic Stochastic General Equilibrium' model were the foundation of the OECD's optimistic forecasts in June 2007. Two months later, the crisis commenced.

That's the negative case against linear models, and equilibrium-oriented models in particular. The positive case for the nonlinear, complex systems approach in economics is the fact that the core phenomena that caused the crisis can be generated by a very simple, fundamentally nonlinear, complex systems model of the economy, which I first developed in 1992 (Keen 1995). This model motivated me to warn that a crisis was imminent from December of 2005 (Bezemer 2010; Fullbrook 2010). Despite its simplicity and stylized nature – or rather because of it, like Lorenz's model of the weather shown in figure 3.3 – it captures the essential features of the real economy in the lead-up to the crisis:

- the magnitude of economic cycles diminished – a phenomenon which mainstream 'Neoclassical' economists interpreted as a good thing, and for which then Federal Reserve Vice-Chairman Ben Bernanke took the credit, on behalf of the Federal Reserve and the Neoclassical economists who dominate it (Bernanke 2004a);
- the distribution of income shifted away from the poor (workers) and towards the rich (bankers), which economists observed but could not explain (nor did they care much about it); and
- the level of private debt rose compared to GDP, which they also ignored.

I built this model to express the ideas of one of the great non-Neoclassical economists, Hyman Minsky, after whom the program *Minsky* was named.

3.1 A complex systems model of economic instability

Minsky developed his theory of systemic instability in capitalism by asking a simple question: 'Can "It" – a Great Depression – happen again?'. To answer this question, Minsky reasoned that 'it is necessary to have an economic theory which makes great depressions one of the possible states in which our type of capitalist economy can find itself' (Minsky 1982, p. xi). His verbal model focused upon the dual role of private debt of both enabling investment in excess of profits, and constituting a burden to investment when debt was too high relative to income. He put it this way:

> The natural starting place for analyzing the relation between debt and income is to take an economy with a cyclical past

that is now doing well ... As the period over which the economy does well lengthens, two things become evident in board rooms. Existing debts are easily validated and units that were heavily in debt prospered; it paid to lever ... As a result, over a period in which the economy does well, views about acceptable debt structure change ... As this continues the economy is transformed into a boom economy.

Stable growth is inconsistent with the manner in which investment is determined in an economy in which debt-financed ownership of capital assets exists, and the extent to which such debt financing can be carried is market determined. *It follows that the fundamental instability of a capitalist economy is upward. The tendency to transform doing well into a speculative investment boom is the basic instability in a capitalist economy.* (Minsky 1982, p. 66, emphasis added)

The basic causal process that Minsky envisaged was that:

- in the aftermath of a recession, both firms and banks are conservative about debt; therefore only conservatively estimated projects receive funding;
- because of this conservative leverage, most projects succeed – leading to firms and banks becoming more adventurous;
- additional borrowing finances more investment, and the economy booms, but private debt also grows;
- the boom drives up wages and raw material costs, reducing profits at the peak of the boom;
- investment falls, and the economy enters another recession;
- wages and raw material prices fall, restoring profitability, but at a higher level of debt than before; and
- the cycle repeats, until ultimately debt is so high that interest on debt exceeds profits, and the economy enters a Great Depression.

This process can be captured in an extremely simple causal chain:

1. Capital *determines* Output;[3]
2. Output *determines* Employment;
3. The rate of employment *determines* the *rate of change* of wages;
4. Output minus Wages and Interest payments *determines* profit;
5. The profit rate *determines* the level of investment,[4] which is the *change in Capital* – which takes us back to the beginning of this causal chain; and
6. The difference between investment and profits *determines* the *change in (private) debt*.

With *Minsky*, or any other system dynamics program, we can turn this step-by-step verbal chain into a mathematical model. Surprisingly, though no assumptions are made about cycles or income distribution in this verbal chain, the real-world phenomena of rising debt, diminishing and then rising cycles, and shifting income distribution from the poor (workers) to the rich (bankers) all emerge in a simulation of this model (see figure 3.4).

What you're witnessing is an instance of a common phenomenon in complex systems models: 'emergent properties', properties which the model displays, but which weren't built into the model by its assumptions or formulas. Instead, they 'emerge' from the interactions of the system's variables: in this case, the employment rate, the wages share of GDP and the level of private debt relative to GDP.

The two key emergent properties of this model are that:

- even though workers do no borrowing in this simple model, they are the ones who effectively pay for the higher level of debt, via a fall in their share of GDP, while that going to capitalists remains constant – inequality rises because the increase in (relatively rich) bankers' share of income is equal to the fall in the (relatively poor) workers' share; and
- cycles diminish and appear to disappear, only to return later and become more and more extreme.

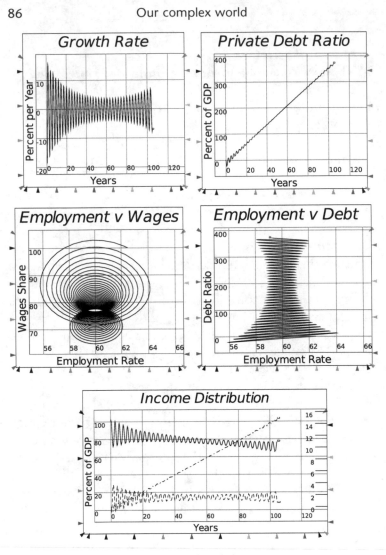

Figure 3.4. The *Keen-Minsky* model and the 'intermittent route to chaos'. See http://www.profstevekeen.com/minsky/

What causes these two emergent properties – the fact that workers, rather than firms, end up paying for the higher level of debt; and the phenomenon of falling and then rising cycles?

The first property occurs because this model is driven by the desire of capitalists to invest, as manifest in the investment equation, where the rate of profit determines the share of investment in total GDP. This implies some rate of profit at which investment precisely equals profit: in the simulations here, that's a 4.3 per cent rate of profit, or a 12.9 per cent share of GDP going to capitalists. That leaves 87.1 per cent of GDP to be divided between workers and bankers, and it doesn't matter to capitalists how that is allocated between them. The dynamics of the model then push income towards bankers and away from workers.

Employment rises as the economy starts to boom because of higher investment, and this ultimately leads to a high rate of employment, which drives up wages. Since investment in excess of profits is debt-financed, the debt ratio also rises during the boom, so that debt servicing costs rise as well. These rising wage and interest costs ultimately mean that the profits expected by capitalists when the boom began are not realized. The increased share of output going to workers and bankers leaves less than capitalists had expected as profits. Investment falls, the rate of growth of the economy falters, and the boom gives way to a slump.

The slump reverses the dynamics that the boom set in train, but doesn't quite reverse the impact of the boom on private debt. Aggregate demand falls, leading to falling employment and declining wages; but at the same time, lower cash flows after the crisis mean that actual debt servicing falls short of what was planned. The recovery from the crisis thus leaves a residue of unpaid debt.

The profit share of output ultimately returns to a level that once again sets off another period of euphoric expectations and high debt-financed investment, but this starts from a higher level of debt relative to GDP than before. With a higher level of debt, the larger share of income going to bankers leaves a lower share for workers. So the workers pay the price for the higher debt level in terms of a lower wages share of GDP, even though they do no borrowing themselves.

Mathematicians know the second emergent property – of cycles diminishing and then growing larger as the crisis approaches – as the 'intermittent route to chaos'. It was first discovered in fluid dynamics (Pomeau and Manneville 1980) in the analysis of Lorenz's weather model, which we discussed earlier. It can only be fully explained mathematically, but I'll try my best in words here. If you don't have mathematical training, this might be a good point to take a coffee break.

A critical part of the phenomenon of complex or 'chaotic' behaviour is the 'nonlinearity' of the model. Because the model has terms involving the multiplication of one system state by another – say, the debt ratio multiplied by the workers' share of GDP – the effect of this interaction is very different when the model is far from an equilibrium than when it is close to it. A long way from the equilibrium, the product of the difference of each of these variables from their equilibrium values is very big: this can, in some circumstances, push the system back towards the equilibrium. But as they approach the equilibrium, the magnitude of this product falls very quickly – in the same way that x squared is much bigger than x when x is greater than one, but much smaller than x when x is less than one: x squared is 4 when x is 2, but ¼ when x is ½. So, far from equilibrium, the nonlinear terms in a model dominate the linear terms, whereas close to the equilibrium, the linear terms dominate the nonlinear ones.[5]

This means, rather paradoxically, that while the nonlinear terms mean that a nonlinear model behaves very differently far from equilibrium, the linear terms determine the stability of an equilibrium.[6] This is why the behaviour of a nonlinear model is very different from the fundamentally linear models that Neoclassicals typically build: in a linear model, if the equilibrium is a 'repeller' – if it pushes the system away, rather than pulling it closer – then it is a repeller far from equilibrium, as well as close to it. That will inevitably mean that the model gets pushed beyond its sensible bounds: you get negative quantities of goods, or negative prices, which are meaningless in an economic model.

But in a nonlinear model, the behaviour near the equilibrium can be very different from the behaviour far from it. If the equilibrium is a repeller close up – where the linear terms dominate – then it can also be an attractor far away – where the nonlinear terms dominate. This is why a complex system can fluctuate indefinitely – it doesn't have to converge to equilibrium.

Things get more complicated still when you delve into the nature of the forces pushing or pulling the system around. Estimated in proximity to a model's equilibria, these are called 'eigenvalues' and 'eigenvectors', in which 'eigen' is a German word meaning 'characteristic'. Eigen*values* tell you how strong the forces are pulling the system towards an equilibrium, or pushing away from it, and eigen*vectors* tell you the orientation of that push or pull.

Eigenvalues are derived by putting the system's equations into a matrix, and then expressing the forces applied to a position close to the equilibria of the matrix equation as a polynomial – an equation in x, x^2, x^3 and so on. Factoring this equation with just the terms in x gives you the eigenvalues of a model. They can be positive, in which case they 'repel' the system from its equilibrium, or negative, in which case they attract, or 'complex', in which case they cause cycles. Complex numbers are the factors of quadratic terms like, for example, (x^2+1), where the roots involve the square root of minus one.

The complex eigenvalues – which cause cyclical behaviour – also have a real number in them, which can be negative, positive or zero. If the real number is negative, the cycle will converge to the equilibrium; if it is positive, the system will diverge from the equilibrium; if it is zero, the system will cycle around the equilibrium, but neither move closer to it nor further away.

The overall behaviour of a model near an equilibrium depends on the interaction of all its eigenvalues, and the most important issue here is the sign of the largest real number, which identifies the system's 'dominant' eigenvalue. If this is negative, then the equilibrium is stable, and if the system starts near enough to the equilibrium, it will converge to it over time. If it is positive, however, then the equilibrium is unstable, and the system will diverge from it over time. The balance of forces also depends on how far the system is from an equilibrium, which is defined in terms of its 'basin of attraction' and 'Lyapunov function' (see Grasselli and Costa Lima 2012 for an example of applying this stability analysis to the model in figure 3.4). As I said, it's complicated (take another coffee break if your head is spinning at this point!).

The model in figure 3.4 has two meaningful equilibria, one of which has been characterized as the 'good equilibrium' (Grasselli and Costa Lima 2012). This has a positive employment rate, a positive wages share of output and a finite debt ratio (the other 'bad equilibrium' has zero employment, zero wages share and an infinite debt ratio). The linearized equation for the good equilibrium has one negative eigenvalue – which means that it attracts the system towards the equilibrium – and one pair of complex eigenvalues (they always come in pairs). For low values of the parameter that gives the slope of the investment function, these complex eigenvalues have zero as their real part. This makes zero the 'dominant eigenvalue' – since zero is bigger than a negative number – but because zero neither attracts nor repels, the negative real eigenvalue can still push the system towards the equilibrium over time.

However, for larger values of the slope of the investment function, the real part of the complex eigenvalues becomes positive, and then it's 'game over' for the stability of the 'good equilibrium'. When the system is sufficiently far away from the equilibrium, the nonlinear forces dominate, dragging the system from its starting point (its 'initial conditions') towards the equilibrium, and the magnitude of the cycles falls as well. But as the system approaches the equilibrium, the linear forces dominate, and the positive component of the complex eigenvalue dominates the negative component of the real eigenvalue. The system starts to move away from the equilibrium, and the cycles get bigger, not smaller. That's what we see in the model shown in figure 3.4, and I saw this phenomenon in a simulation of my original model, before I worked out its stability characteristics using the techniques described here (Grasselli and Costa Lima 2012; Keen 1995, 2020b).[7]

This was *not* a prediction of Minsky's verbal model: though he had famously written that 'Stability – or tranquility – in a world with a cyclical past and capitalist financial institutions is destabilizing' (Minsky 1978, p. 10), this was in reference to a single cycle, not the pattern of cycles over time. When I first constructed this model in August 1992, this phenomenon of falling and then rising cycles was in many ways its most surprising feature, and I ended the paper with what I thought at the time was a great rhetorical flourish:

> From the perspective of economic theory and policy, this vision of a capitalist economy with finance requires us to go beyond that habit of mind that Keynes described so well, the excessive reliance on the (stable) recent past as a guide to the future. The chaotic dynamics explored in this paper should warn us against accepting a period of relative tranquility in a capitalist economy as anything other than a lull before the storm. (Keen 1995, p. 634)

Then, much to my amazement at the time, the real world began to emulate my model. Each new recession after 1980 came with a lower peak level of unemployment (Komlos 2021),[8] and each new boom with a lower peak level of inflation, while the level of private debt rose far faster than GDP (see figure 3.5).

With their linear, equilibrium-fixated approach to modelling, Neoclassical economists saw this phenomenon as a vindication of their economic theory and the policies

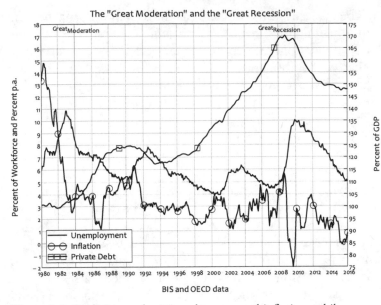

Figure 3.5. Declining cycles in employment and inflation, while private debt rises

based upon it, and extrapolated this trend forward in their models. They labelled the decline in economic volatility the 'Great Moderation', and attributed it to their economic policies, which emphasized reducing inflation using Federal Reserve control of short-term interest rates. Ben Bernanke, then a member of the Federal Reserve Board of Governors, was particularly effusive in his praise for 'the Great Moderation':

> As it turned out, the low-inflation era of the past two decades has seen not only significant improvements in economic growth and productivity but also a marked *reduction* in economic volatility, both in the United States and abroad, a phenomenon that has been dubbed 'the Great Moderation.' Recessions have become less frequent and milder, and quarter-to-quarter volatility in output and employment has declined significantly as well ... there is evidence for the view that improved control of inflation has

contributed in important measure to *this welcome change in the economy.* (Bernanke 2004b, emphasis added)

My reaction, in contrast, was that this pattern, which emulated my simple model, was the harbinger of a future crisis. That crisis arrived in late 2007, and it was, before Covid-19, the most serious economic crisis since the Great Depression. Unemployment shot up above the level of all previous post-war recessions,[9] while inflation gave way to deflation.

Neoclassical economists were caught totally unawares by this crisis, and in the aftermath to it there were some admissions that their models had weaknesses. But they could see no alternative to their core approach, which was to attempt to derive macroeconomic models from the foundation of microeconomics – a practice that they describe as 'microfoundations'.

> The pursuit of a widely accepted analytical macroeconomic core, in which to locate discussions and extensions, may be a pipe dream, but it is a dream surely worth pursuing ... Starting from explicit microfoundations is clearly essential; where else to start from? (Blanchard 2016)

The belief that macroeconomics had to be derived from microeconomics took hold in the 1980s, as the previously dominant 'IS-LM' macroeconomic models were replaced by 'Real Business Cycle' models, which were directly derived from microeconomic concepts of utility-maximizing consumers and profit-maximizing firms. As then President of the American Economic Association Robert Lucas put it, 'Nobody was satisfied with IS-LM as the end of macroeconomic theorizing. The idea was we were going to tie it together with microeconomics and that was the job of our generation' (Lucas 2004, p. 20).

Complexity theory has shown that the belief that macroeconomics must be derived from microeconomics is false.

3.2 Complexity and the impossibility of microfoundations

Do yourself a favour: read one of the best and most accessible thought pieces ever penned by a scientist: Physics Nobel Laureate Philip Anderson's 'More is Different' (Anderson 1972).[10] The paper itself arose in a methodological dispute within physics over the role of 'reductionism' in science. This is the practice of understanding a complicated field by breaking it down into its constituent parts, understanding them independently, and then building your knowledge of the whole from the parts. Anderson acknowledged the success of reductionism in enabling us to develop modern science, but he pointed out that reductionism does not imply 'constructionism':

> The ability to reduce everything to simple fundamental laws does not imply the ability to start from those laws and reconstruct the universe. (Anderson 1972, p. 393)

Speaking as one of the original researchers who discovered complex systems phenomena in science, Anderson noted that while 'constructionism' works for simple systems with simple (often linear) relationships between their parts,

> The constructionist hypothesis breaks down when confronted with the twin difficulties of scale and complexity. The behavior of large and complex aggregates of elementary particles, it turns out, is not to be understood in terms of a simple extrapolation of the properties of a few particles. Instead, at each level of complexity entirely new properties appear, and the understanding of the new behaviors requires research which I think is as fundamental in its nature as any other. (Anderson 1972, p. 393)

Anderson noted that it was possible to rank sciences according to the principle that 'The elementary entities of science X obey the laws of science Y':

X	Y
Solid state or many-body physics	Elementary particle physics
Chemistry	Many-body physics
Molecular biology	Chemistry
Cell biology	Molecular biology
...	...
Psychology	Physiology
Social Sciences	Psychology

But this hierarchy does not imply that science X is 'just applied Y.' At each stage entirely new laws, concepts, and generalizations are necessary, requiring inspiration and creativity to just as great a degree as in the previous one. Psychology is not applied biology, nor is biology applied chemistry. (Anderson 1972, p. 393)

Mainstream economists, however, are driven by the belief that macroeconomics should be 'just applied microeconomics': making it so has been their research agenda for the last thirty years.

In general, this is foolhardy: imagine, for example, that the same belief took over biology, so that biologists believed that 'Molecular Biology is just applied Chemistry'. Then a valid Molecular Biology laboratory project would be 'Create life from its fundamental chemicals'. Of course, that's impossible: despite all the knowledge chemists have of chemistry today, and biologists of biology, no-one knows how to turn chemicals into a life form, though clearly this happened in the distant past on Earth (Cornell et al. 2019). Therefore, Biology cannot be reduced to 'Applied Chemistry': if Chemists did in fact insist that Biology must meet this standard, then there would be no science of Biology at all.

In particular in economics, *economists* have already shown that this objective – to reduce macroeconomics to applied microeconomics – is impossible. In a well-known but misleadingly interpreted result called the

Sonnenschein–Mantel–Debreu theorem (Arrow et al. 1981–1993; Gorman 1953; Kihlstrom et al. 1976; Shafer and Sonnenschein 1982; Sonnenschein 1973a, 1973b), mathematical economists posed the question 'is it possible to derive a downward-sloping market demand curve by aggregating the demand curves of numerous individuals, all of whom have downward-sloping individual demand curves?'. Their answer was that it was not, *unless* you assumed, to quote the first economist to derive this result, that 'the Engel curves for different individuals at the same prices are parallel straight lines' (Gorman 1953, p. 63). Gorman unpacked his economic jargon with this telling assertion:

> The necessary and sufficient condition quoted above is intuitively reasonable. It says, in effect, that an extra unit of purchasing power should be spent in the same way no matter to whom it is given. (Gorman 1953, p. 64)

There is nothing 'intuitively reasonable' about that condition: it is saying that Elon Musk will spend an extra dollar buying the same things that a homeless person would buy with that dollar.[11] This is obviously untrue, and *intuitively unreasonable*: why does Gorman claim the exact opposite?

It is because, if the distribution of income does affect consumption – and it obviously does – then the market demand curve that can be derived by summing the downward-sloping individual demand curves of numerous individuals can have any shape at all:[12] it does not have to be downward sloping. With that discovery, the whole theory of 'supply and demand' dies. As other researchers in this field put it, 'The utility hypothesis tells us nothing about market demand unless it is augmented by additional requirements' (Shafer and Sonnenschein 1982, p. 672).

This is a classic 'emergent property'. Not only can macroeconomics not be derived from microeconomics, even the model of a market demand curve can't be derived

– with the properties Neoclassical economists want it to have – from the model of a single consumer. The quest for a microeconomics foundation for macroeconomics is futile.

But a quest for firm foundations does make sense: what might they be?

3.3 The macrofoundations of macroeconomics

In what may seem a paradox, macroeconomics can be derived directly from itself.

Macroeconomics is about economic aggregates, and much of it involves ratios of one aggregate to another. We worry about the rate of unemployment, which is the ratio of those unemployed to the workforce; income distribution is concerned with how much of income goes to particular groups, compared to total income; even the rate of economic growth is the ratio of the change in GDP to its current level. These macroeconomic aggregates and their ratios define the subject, and a dynamic macroeconomics can be derived by simply converting these definitions into statements about change over time.

In other words, *the structure of the economy largely determines how it behaves.* This structure is codified to a substantial extent in macroeconomic definitions themselves. By simply taking core definitions and turning them into dynamic statements, we can build the foundations of macroeconomics. As we expand the definitions – for example, by going beyond treating GDP as a simple number and consider a range of industries producing a range of products – then the mathematical form of that expanded definition will give us a richer model still. There is no need to drill down to microeconomics, let alone build up from it towards macroeconomics – and as I explain in *Debunking Economics* (Keen 2011), virtually all of conventional microeconomics is bunk anyway.

Consider the model of Minsky's 'Financial Instability Hypothesis' shown in figure 3.4. The three key ratios in that model are the employment rate, the wages share of GDP and the debt ratio:

$$Employment_{Rate} = \frac{Labour}{Population}$$
$$Wage_{Share} = \frac{Wages}{GDP}$$
$$Debt_{Ratio} = \frac{Debt}{GDP} \qquad (3.1)$$

As they stand, these are 'static' definitions: they define ratios that are true for all time, but they don't describe the process of change of those ratios through time. However, we can derive statements about that process of change by 'simply' differentiating them with respect to time.

Well, that's simple for people who 'speak' mathematics, but if you don't, there's another simple trick using percentages that makes this easy: *the percentage rate of change of a ratio is equal to the percentage rate of change of the numerator, minus the percentage rate of change of the denominator.* Similarly, *the percentage rate of change of a product* (say, Wages defined as the Wage Rate times Labour) *is the sum of the percentage rates of change of the two parts of the product.*

So, just by looking at the definitions shown in equation (3.1), we can write them in a dynamic form:

- The percentage rate of change of the Employment Rate is equal to the percentage rate of change of the Labour force, minus the percentage rate of growth of Population;
- The percentage rate of change of the Wages Share of GDP is the percentage rate of change of Wages, minus the percentage rate of change of GDP; and
- The percentage rate of change of the Debt Ratio is the percentage rate of change of Debt, minus the percentage rate of change of GDP.

Using the same functions for wage change and investment as in figure 3.4, and the same assumption that debt finances investment in excess of profits, this leads to a model which has precisely the same dynamics. There are issues with some of these definitions which would need to be addressed in more sophisticated models[13] (Harcourt 1972; Robinson 1964, 1971a, 1971b; Samuelson 1966; Sraffa 1960),[14] but just as Lorenz's highly stylized model of turbulence is a key foundation of modern meteorology, the model we have developed here is a key foundation for a genuinely modern macroeconomics – and not one scintilla of microeconomic reasoning was involved.

It was also a relatively easy exercise to construct this model, compared to the painful process that Neoclassical economists must go through, using their invalid 'micro-foundations' approach, to build even the simplest of their equilibrium-fixated Real Business Cycle models – let alone their attempt at greater realism with 'Dynamic Stochastic General Equilibrium' models. As the leading Neoclassical modeller Olivier Blanchard put it:

> Thinking in terms of a set of distortions to a competitive economy implies a long slog from the competitive model to a reasonably plausible description of the economy. But, again, it is hard to see where else to start from. (Blanchard 2018, p. 47)

No such unnecessary hard work is required to build this model, and it can be extended by generalizing the definitions used. For example, the impact of inflation can be considered by replacing 'real' GDP as used here with nominal GDP, where real GDP equals nominal GDP divided by the Price level. The rate of inflation then turns up in two of the model's three equations. The abstraction of a single number for GDP can be replaced by the reality that it is really the sum of the outputs of numerous different industries. Non-productive 'Ponzi' uses of debt can be introduced alongside debt being used to finance investment. Government spending can be introduced – a topic we explored in the previous chapter – and so on. Macroeconomics can guide its own development, once we abandon the constructionist fallacy that it should be derived from microeconomics.

If a foundational layer for macroeconomics is sought, it should be a link with the fundamental physics of how our civilization transforms the mineral and biological gifts the biosphere provides into the industrial products we consume, and the waste we necessarily dump back into the biosphere. That has not been done, and largely cannot be done, by Neoclassical economists.

4
Economics, energy and the environment

Most economists treat Adam Smith as 'the father of economics'. I disagree. Though I appreciate some of Smith's work, I primarily regard him as the person most responsible for causing economics to deviate from the physically realistic approach that economics should have taken, which was established by his intellectual predecessors, the Physiocrats.

The key difference between Smith and these long-forgotten pre-Classical economists were their respective views about how output and wealth are created. This is obvious when one compares the very first sentences of Smith's *The Wealth of Nations* (Smith 1776) to Cantillon's *An Essay on Economic Theory* (Cantillon 1755). Cantillon attributed all wealth to land:

> Land is the source or matter from which all wealth is drawn; man's labor provides the form for its production, and wealth in itself is nothing but the food, conveniences, and pleasures of life. (Cantillon 1755, p. 21)

Smith, using *very* similar language, attributed the wealth of nations to labour:

The annual labour of every nation is the fund which origi-
nally supplies it with all the necessaries and conveniences
of life which it annually consumes. (Smith 1776, p. 10)

Both authors had roles for the other's nominated primary
factor in their analysis. However, by emphasizing labour
over land, Smith set economics on a course which, two
centuries later, resulted in models of production in which
output is treated as being generated by labour and capital
alone. Neoclassicals use the 'Cobb–Douglas Production
Function' (Cobb and Douglas 1928), in which output is
produced by a flexible combination of labour and capital;
Post Keynesians use the 'Leontief Production Function', in
which output is proportional to the fraction of the capital
stock that is in use.[1] Neither have any explicit role for
inputs from outside the economy, from the natural world
which existed long before humans did – let alone humanity's modern industrial society.

The Physiocratic approach, in contrast, asserted that
without the 'free gift' of Nature (Turgot 1774, p. 16),
there would be no production at all. Though this could
not be known at the time, from the point of view of
modern physics, the Physiocrats were correct and Smith
was wrong – and so too, therefore, are modern models
of production, because they pretend that output can be
produced without inputs from nature, and also, without
waste. Both these beliefs are fallacies, according to the
Laws of Thermodynamics.[2]

The key 'free gift of Nature' is energy: without energy,
not only can no work be done, life itself can't exist. Figure
4.1 illustrates the basic principle: useful work can be done
if there is a gap between the heat of a source of energy and
its environment, and only if that environment is at absolute
zero can all the energy in the source be turned into useful
work. Waste can be minimized, but not eliminated: it is
inevitable when energy is used to perform useful work.

Though the laws are difficult to understand, their impact
is not: any theory which violates them is false. This was

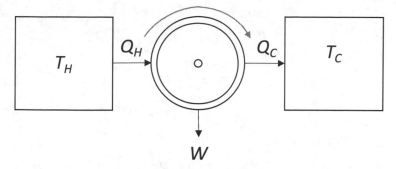

Figure 4.1. The basic principle of a heat engine: Work can be done if $T_H > T_C$

put beautifully by the early twentieth-century physicist Arthur Eddington, when he abstractly considered theories that violate the most mind-bending of these laws, the Second Law, that the degree of disorder of a closed system – known as its 'entropy' – necessarily rises over time:

> The law that entropy always increases holds, I think, the supreme position among the laws of Nature. If someone points out to you that your pet theory of the universe is in disagreement with Maxwell's equations – then so much the worse for Maxwell's equations. If it is found to be contradicted by observation – well, these experimentalists do bungle things sometimes. But if your theory is found to be against the Second Law of Thermodynamics I can give you no hope; there is nothing for it but to collapse in deepest humiliation. (Eddington 1928, p. 27)

Economics has violated these laws ever since the Physiocrats, whose correct speculations about production emanating from the 'free gift of Nature' actually predate the invention of the word 'energy' by half a century (Smith 1998). This ignorance has persisted despite the staggeringly tight correlation that exists between global energy use and global GDP (see figure 4.2).[3]

Therefore, if you don't explicitly – or at least implicitly – capture the role of energy in production in your economic

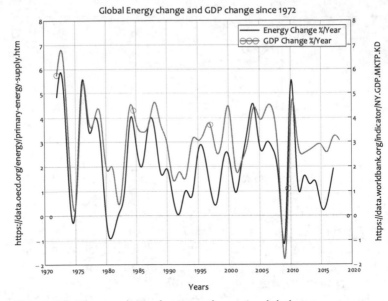

Figure 4.2. The correlation between change in global energy consumption and change in global GDP is 0.83

model, your economic model is wrong, both theoretically and empirically. At the very least, energy *must* be included in economic models of production (including the models shown in the previous chapter of this book), in a manner that is consistent with the Laws of Thermodynamics. And yet, to date, apart from the work of iconoclasts like Boulding (Boulding 1973, 1992), Georgescu-Roegen (Georgescu-Roegen 1970, 1979, 1986), Daly (Daly 1991a, 2009), Smil (Smil 1987, 2017), Hall (Hall et al. 2001; Hall and Day 2009) and Kümmel, Ayres and colleagues (Ayres 1978; Ayres and Voudouris 2014; Ayres et al. 2013; Kümmel 2011; Kümmel et al. 2010, 2015), economics has effectively ignored the role of energy in production.

An insight that occurred to me in 2016, while I was staying at Bob Ayres's house in Paris – which was full of sculptures – led to a simple way to overcome this weakness: 'capital without energy is a sculpture' and 'labour without energy is a corpse' (Keen et al. 2019,

p. 41). Without energy, a machine is just a static object that can do nothing. With energy, the machine, managed by labourers, can perform work, and hence generate what we call GDP. Energy can therefore be incorporated into models of production *simply by treating both labour and capital as means by which energy is harnessed to perform useful work.*[4]

In mathematical terms, the input for 'capital' (or more correctly, the number of machines) in the standard economic models of production should be replaced by the 'number' of machines, times the energy consumed by each machine per year, times the efficiency with which that energy is turned into useful work – and the same thing should be done for 'labour' (or the number of hours worked per year). When this is applied to both the Neoclassical Cobb–Douglas and the Post Keynesian Leontief production functions,[5] it resolves several long-lasting conundrums in economics.

These models now correctly state the importance of energy in production. In contrast, the way in which Neoclassical economists have attempted to incorporate energy into the Cobb–Douglas production function – by tacking energy on as a third, independent input on the same footing as labour and capital (Stiglitz 1974a, 1974b) – implied that if energy input dropped by 80 per cent, output would fall by a mere 8 per cent. This was justifiably ridiculed by Larry Summers:

> There'd be a set of economists who'd sit around explaining that electricity was only four percent of the economy, and so if you lost eighty percent of electricity you couldn't possibly have lost more than three percent of the economy, and there'd be people in Minnesota and Chicago and stuff who'd be writing that paper … but it would be stupid. (Summers 2013)

With the energy-modified Cobb–Douglas function (shown in footnote 5 to this chapter), and standard values for its coefficient, output would fall 33 per cent if energy input fell by 80 per cent. This still seriously understates what would actually happen, but it is at least in the right ballpark. With the energy-modified Leontief function, the fall in output is identical to the fall in energy, which is clearly consistent with the data shown in figure 4.2, where there is an almost 1 for 1 relationship between changes in GDP and changes in energy.

The stunning – but, from the point of view of the Laws of Thermodynamics, utterly expected (Garrett 2012a, 2012b, 2014; Garrett et al. 2020)[6] – correlation between change in energy and change in GDP shown in figure 4.2 also provides a strong reason to reject the Cobb–Douglas function and prefer the Leontief. The Cobb–Douglas function's exponent is normally derived from income distribution data, and reflects the profit share in GDP. There are numerous theoretical problems with this derivation (McCombie 1998, 2000; Shaikh 1974, 2005; Sraffa 1960), and Mankiw added a strong empirical problem as well when he pointed out that, with this conventional exponent, the cross-country predictions that the Cobb–Douglas model makes are wildly at variance with the empirical data:

> the model can explain incomes that vary by a multiple of slightly more than two. Yet income per person varies by a multiple of more than ten ... the model predicts convergence at about twice the rate that actually occurs ... the profit rate ... should be about 1,000 percent per year in poor countries. (Mankiw et al. 1995, pp. 283, 285, 287)

Mankiw notes that these problems disappear if the coefficient for capital is of the order of two-thirds rather than one-third, and for other reasons he recommends a coefficient of 0.8. At this level, the Cobb–Douglas function makes much more realistic predictions about the impact of a reduction in energy inputs on economic output: for example, it predicts a 1.6 per cent fall in GDP for a 2 per cent fall in energy consumption. But the much simpler Leontief model, using coefficients derived from the empirical fit shown in figure 4.2, implies a 2 per cent fall in GDP from a 2 per cent fall in energy inputs. This is a much better fit to the data from a much simpler model, which, via Occam's Razor, implies that the more complicated Cobb–Douglas function should be dispensed with in favour of the Leontief.

The empirical failure of the Cobb–Douglas model arises from what its proponents see as its greatest strength: it implies the possibility of substituting one input for another, which the Leontief model does not do. That was hypothetically a strength over the Leontief model when labour and capital were the only inputs considered: it's possible to imagine substituting many workers for one machine (say, workers using shovels versus an excavator). *But there is no substitute for energy.* Energy can be used more efficiently, but this has limits, and efficiency of energy use is included in the modified Leontief equation anyway.

The modified production equations also necessarily express the generation of waste. Since the equations include a term for the efficiency with which energy input is turned into useful work, the balance of that energy is waste energy. The same thing applies when matter is included: if energy is used to convert raw materials into useful materials, then production also generates waste materials. This forges a fundamental link between economics and ecology, in place of the Neoclassical treatment of pollution as an 'externality', which can hypothetically be reduced to zero with appropriate property rights and pricing (Coase 1988; Major et al. 2016). To produce output we *must* create waste; waste can be minimized but not completely eliminated, and it *must* be dumped into the biosphere – at least while production occurs only on Planet Earth – otherwise there can be no production. Equally, production requires physical resources from the environment, which is omitted from modern Neoclassical models, but which can be incorporated into the Goodwin-based models used in

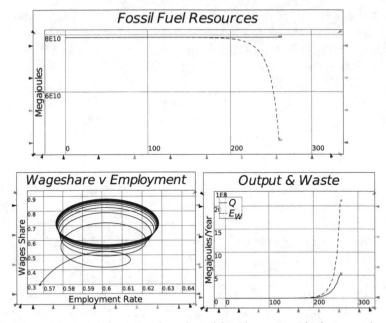

Figure 4.3. A simple energy-based model with resource depletion and waste production. See http://www.profstevekeen.com/minsky/

chapter 3 (see figure 4.3), which incorporates a resource constraint into a Goodwin model in which energy is the essential input to production.

Bringing energy into models of production also resolves the long-running dispute over what is the source of economic growth over time – the surplus of outputs over inputs – with an existential answer: *there is no surplus.* Marx's use of the Classical approach to economics, to argue that 'surplus value' arose from the difference between the value of the wage workers were paid and the value of the goods they produced, played a major role in motivating the overthrow of the Classical School by the Neoclassical in the late nineteenth century. The Neoclassical riposte was that labour and capital together were responsible for the increase in utility from increasing production over time. Post Keynesian economists simply accepted that a surplus was produced, as did economists inspired by Piero Sraffa (Sraffa 1960), without speculating about what gave rise to it (Backhouse 1988; Hamouda and Harcourt 1988).

All of these explanations fall foul of the Laws of Thermodynamics. Production can be viewed as a decrease in entropy, or an increase in order: we take raw materials and convert them into finished goods, with (outside of recessions and crises like Covid-19) both the number and the sophistication of the goods rising over time. This is only possible because we are exploiting existing sources of energy – which, by the First Law, we can neither create nor destroy – to cause a decrease in entropy in our system of production. This decrease in entropy, when our frame of reference is the economy, is only possible because of the overall increase in entropy, when our frame of reference is the Universe.

Production, given the Second Law of Thermodynamics, is thus fundamentally an operation that produces a deficit (an *increase* in entropy, or 'disorder'), rather than a surplus. Rather than capitalists exploiting workers, as Marx argued, or capital and labour jointly causing a rise in utility over time, as Neoclassicals assert, humanity's social classes compete for a share in the useful work created by the exploitation of pre-existing energy – primarily, the planet's fossil fuel reserves.

4.1 Our unsustainable future

This was never a sustainable situation. If you think otherwise – if you are, perhaps, a climate change sceptic (many economists are) – then consider this argument by a physicist (Murphy 2012). As our economies grow, their use of energy grows.[7] With continued growth, we were bound to alter the planet so much that our economy would end up destroying life on Earth – *and this has nothing to do with global warming*. It is instead a consequence of the Laws of Thermodynamics.

By the Second Law, using energy to perform useful work necessitates a predictable amount of waste energy generation. At a sustained rate of global economic growth of 2.3 per cent per annum – which is generally considered too low today, since it would lead to continually rising unemployment – the waste energy would increase the temperature of the surface of the Earth to 100°C some time in the twenty-fifth century:[8]

> at a 2.3% growth rate (conveniently chosen to represent a 10× increase every century), we would reach boiling temperature in about 400 years. (Murphy 2012)

Needless to say, life on Earth would have ended by then, and capitalism well before that. The only way growth could be sustained for more than another two centuries from today would be if humanity became 'a multi-planetary species', to quote Elon Musk (Musk 2017). That could very conceivably happen before the Laws of Thermodynamics drive us extinct. But with global warming, we don't have the luxury of centuries. We may barely even have decades.

We have reached the point vividly described by Kenneth Boulding almost thirty years ago, of a 'spaceman economy', rather than the 'cowboy economy' in which capitalism originated:

> The closed earth of the future requires economic principles which are somewhat different from those of the open earth of the past. For the sake of picturesqueness, I am tempted to call the open economy the 'cowboy economy,' the cowboy being symbolic of the illimitable plains and also associated with reckless, exploitative, romantic, and violent behavior, which is characteristic of open societies. The closed economy of the future might similarly be called the 'spaceman' economy, in which the earth has become a single spaceship, without unlimited reservoirs of anything, either for extraction or for pollution, and in which, therefore, man must find his place in a cyclical ecological

system which is capable of continuous reproduction of material form even though it cannot escape having inputs of energy. (Boulding 1992)

Regrettably, we have reached this point blindly, since, of all the schools of thought throughout the history of economics, only the Physiocrats had a theory of value which was consistent with the Laws of Thermodynamics. Though the Physiocrats erred in believing that only agriculture received the 'free gift of Nature' – when today we know that manufacturing and services also exploit the free gift of energy via fossil fuels, nuclear and solar energy – they were correct in seeing production as being fundamentally based on turning what Nature provides 'for free' into commodities for sale. I pine for the economics that could have developed had Cantillon, Turgot and Quesnay provided the foundations of economics, rather than Adam Smith:

> the produce of the land divides into two parts. The one comprehends the subsistence and the profits of the husbandman, which are the rewards for his labour, and the conditions on which he agrees to cultivate the field of the proprietor; the other which remains, is that independent and disposable part, *which the earth produces as a free gift to the proprietor over and above what he has disbursed*; and it is out of this share of the proprietor's, or what is called the revenue, that he is enabled to live without labour, and which he can carry where ever he will. (Turgot 1774, pp. 9, 15–16, emphasis added)

An economics built on these foundations could easily have had its error of attributing all wealth to agriculture corrected, once physicists had developed an understanding of energy. It would have correctly anticipated a future world, far from the 'cowboy economy' in which economic theory originated, when accumulated pollution and resource depletion could undermine both production and the biosphere itself. Economists would have expected continued growth to lead to ecological problems – and their warnings would have been far more sophisticated than that provided by Malthus (Malthus 1798). Economics would have warned us of the dangers of exponential growth on a finite planet long before the process became a threat to the continued existence of capitalism.

Instead, when ecological problems started to become evident in the 1970s, economics was dominated by the Neoclassical school, which had by then eliminated most, if not all, of the contrary perspective provided by Keynes. All the failings of Neoclassical economics detailed in this book then turned up in their work, which has vastly underestimated the dangers of climate change. Given the primary role that economists have in shaping economic policy, this has caused us to behave as 'Wild West' cowboys when we are instead residents of the very precarious 'Spaceship Earth'.

I can say only one thing in favour of the work by Neoclassical economists on climate change: it is so bad that, once it becomes obvious how serious a threat climate change is, revulsion at how Neoclassical economists have trivialized the dangers may finally lead to the overthrow of Neoclassical economics itself.

4.2 Revolution by revulsion

I have been a critic of Neoclassical economics since mid-1971, fifty years before the publication of this book. The work done by Neoclassical economists on climate change is, without doubt, the worst work that I have encountered in that half-century (Keen 2020a).

According to these Neoclassical economists, the impact of climate change upon the economy will be trivial. To cite the economics chapter of the 2014 report of the Intergovernmental Panel on Climate Change (IPCC):

> For most economic sectors, the impact of climate change will be small relative to the impacts of other

drivers (*medium evidence, high agreement*). Changes in population, age, income, technology, relative prices, lifestyle, regulation, governance, and many other aspects of socioeconomic development will have an impact on the supply and demand of economic goods and services that is large relative to the impact of climate change. (Arent et al. 2014, p. 662)

Similarly, William Nordhaus, who was awarded the Sveriges Riksbank Prize in Economic Sciences in Memory of Alfred Nobel in 2018 'for integrating climate change into long-run macroeconomic analysis' (Nordhaus 2018a), asserted that a 6°C increase in global temperatures over pre-industrial levels would reduce global economic output by a mere 8.5 per cent, compared to what it would have been in the complete absence of climate change: 'damages are 2.1 percent of global income at 3°C warming and 8.5 percent of income at 6°C warming' (Nordhaus 2018b, p. 345).

In an earlier survey paper, Nordhaus noted that the median prediction of his eighteen respondents – the majority of whom were Neoclassical economists – was that a 3°C increase in temperature by 2090 would cause a 3.6 per cent fall in GDP. Stated in terms of the growth rate between 1991 and 2090, this is a prediction that global warming 'would reduce the growth of per capita incomes from, say, 1.50 percent per year to 1.485 percent per year' (Nordhaus 1994, p. 48). Given the imprecise methods by which economic statistics are constructed, this predicted 0.015 per cent decline in the annual growth rate is too small to measure: as one of his economist-respondents put it, 'I am impressed with the view that it takes a very sharp pencil to see the difference between the world with and without climate change or with and without mitigation' (Nordhaus 1994, p. 48).

These sanguine beliefs bear no resemblance whatsoever to the world that scientists envisage would exist on an Earth 6°C hotter than its pre-industrial self. As climate scientist Tim Lenton observed in 2013, 'There is currently a huge gulf between natural scientists' understanding of climate tipping points and economists' representations of climate catastrophes in integrated assessment models (IAMs)' (Lenton and Ciscar 2013, p. 585). We can get a feel for how huge that gulf is by considering just three issues: the impact of higher global temperatures on human physiology, on the range of the planet that is inhabitable by other species, and on the structure of the atmosphere.

A critical feature of human physiology is our ability to dissipate internal heat by perspiration. To do so, the external air needs to be colder than our ideal body temperature of about 37°C, and dry enough to absorb our perspiration as well. This becomes impossible when the combination of heat and humidity, known as the 'wet bulb temperature', exceeds 35°C. Above this level, we are unable to dissipate the heat generated by our bodies, and the accumulated heat will kill a healthy individual within a few hours. Scientists have estimated that a 3.8°C increase in the global average temperature would make Jakarta's temperature and humidity combination fatal for humans every day of the year, while a 5.5°C increase would mean that *even New York* would experience 55 days per year when the combination of temperature and humidity would be deadly (Mora et al. 2017, fig. 4). In general, with a 5.5°C temperature increase, anywhere between the 'mid-latitudes (for example, 40°N or S) will be exposed to 60 deadly days per year' (Mora et al. 2017, p. 504). That area is currently home to 74 per cent of the world's human population (Mora et al. 2017, p. 501).

Temperature also affects the viable range for all biological organisms on the planet – not just humans. Scientists have estimated that a 4.5°C increase in global temperatures would reduce the area of the planet in which life could exist by 40 per cent or more, with the decline in the liveable area of the planet ranging from a minimum of 30 per cent for mammals to a maximum of 80 per cent for insects (Warren et al. 2018, fig. 1, p. 792).

The Earth's current climate has three major air circulation systems in each hemisphere: a 'Hadley Cell' between the Equator and 30°, a mid-latitude cell between 30° and 60°, and a polar cell between 60° and 90°.[9] This structure is why there are such large differences in temperature between the tropics, temperate and Arctic regions, and relatively small differences within each region.[10] Scientists modelled the stability of these cells, and concluded that they could be tipped, by an average global temperature increase of 4.3°C or more, into a state with just one cell in the Northern Hemisphere, and an average Arctic temperature of 22.5°C. This abrupt transition (known as a bifurcation), some time in the next century, would utterly alter weather patterns everywhere in the Northern Hemisphere, profoundly disrupting all forms of life, and it would occur far too quickly for any meaningful adaptation, by natural and human systems alike (Kypke et al. 2020, fig. 6, p. 399).

These immense physical impacts expected by scientists cannot be reconciled with the trivial economic impacts expected by economists. An Earth that was on average 6°C hotter than pre-industrial levels (about 5°C hotter than today) would be uninhabitable for humans, except perhaps around the Poles, while those survivable regions would lack essential supports for life – such as topsoil for agriculture, which takes thousands of years to develop, in contrast to the century or so over which economists have blithely considered that global temperatures would rise that much (Nordhaus 2018a, Slide 6).

How did this 'huge gulf', as Tim Lenton put it, develop between 'natural scientists' understanding of climate tipping points and economists' representations of climate catastrophes in integrated assessment models' (Lenton and Ciscar 2013, p. 585)? It developed because Neoclassical economists (Nordhaus 2013; Nordhaus and Sztorc 2013) have utterly misconstrued the work of climate scientists on this topic (Lenton et al. 2008).

In 2008, Lenton published the results of a survey of the informed opinions of specialists on major components of the world's climate, to estimate which components could be triggered into a significant qualitative change by increases in temperature that could be expected this century (Lenton et al. 2008). Entitled 'Tipping Elements in the Earth's Climate System', the paper identified eight components that could be triggered, with two of these – Arctic summer sea-ice and the Greenland ice sheet – highly likely to be triggered. The paper's conclusion opened with the following three sentences:

> Society may be lulled into a false sense of security by smooth projections of global change. Our synthesis of present knowledge suggests that a variety of tipping elements could reach their critical point within this century under anthropogenic climate change. The greatest threats are tipping the Arctic sea-ice and the Greenland ice sheet, and at least five other elements could surprise us by exhibiting a nearby tipping point. (Lenton et al. 2008)

Nordhaus summarized these findings as follows in Chapter 5 of his book *The Climate Casino: Risk, Uncertainty, and Economics for a Warming World* (Nordhaus 2013):

> Their review finds no critical tipping elements with a time horizon less than 300 years until global temperatures have increased by at least 3°C. (Nordhaus 2013, p. 60)

In the manual to his DICE model ('Dynamic Integrated Climate Economy'), Nordhaus justified the use of a quadratic for his damages function by this reference to Lenton:

> The current version assumes that damages are a quadratic function of temperature change and does not include sharp thresholds or tipping points, but this is consistent with the survey by Lenton et al. (2008). (Nordhaus and Sztorc 2013, p. 11)

These statements by Nordhaus do not summarize Lenton's conclusions: they contradict them. This affected not just

Nordhaus's own modelling of climate change, but that of the entire, relatively small community of Neoclassical economists working on climate change. Though some papers and models pay lip service to the existence tipping points, all effectively proceed *as if* there will be no tipping points triggered by temperature rises expected this century.

However, the scientific literature is adamant that there will be tipping points in the climate this century, unless drastic action is taken to reduce humanity's generation of CO_2. A follow-up paper to Lenton et al. (2008) concluded not only that 'a planetary threshold in the Earth System could exist at a temperature rise as low as 2°C above preindustrial' temperatures (Steffen et al. 2018, p. 8258), but also that one tipping point could trigger 'tipping cascades', in which one qualitative change (such as the disappearance of Arctic summer sea-ice) could cause amplification effects (such as the Arctic going from predominantly a reflector of solar energy to an absorber) that made other tipping points occur (such as the termination of the 'Gulf Stream' and other ocean currents). This process could push the planet into a 'hothouse Earth' scenario (Steffen et al. 2018, p. 8252) with vastly higher temperatures than today, and a climate no longer conducive to human civilization – and possibly, also not conducive to human life.

The contrast between the research by scientists and the damage estimates made by economists could hardly be starker. The 2014 IPCC Report published a figure showing nineteen estimates by economists of the impact on global income of levels of global warming from 1°C to 5.4°C above pre-industrial temperatures (see figure 4.4). Even the most extreme estimate – of a 12.4 per cent fall in GDP for a 3.2°C increase in temperature (Maddison and Rehdanz 2011) – ignored the issue of tipping points, while all these estimates are trivial compared to what can be inferred from the scientific literature.

There are, of course, no actual data on the relationship between the temperature change due to global warming and GWP ('gross world product' – the planetary sum of

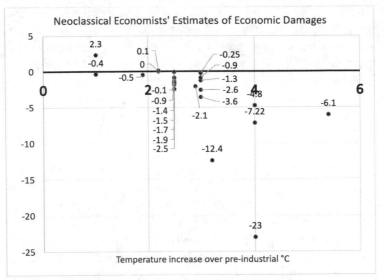

Figure 4.4. Estimates of the total impact of climate change plotted against the assumed climate change.[a] Adapted from Arent et al. (2014, figure 10.1, p. 690)

[a] The 23% fall for a 4°C temperature increase data point comes from Burke et al. (2015), published after the IPCC Report. Even this most severe prediction in the Neoclassical economic literature ignores tipping points.

'gross domestic product'), because global warming of this scale hasn't happened yet. Even the two numbers shown for a 1°C increase – a 2.3 per cent *increase* (Tol 2002) and a 0.4 per cent fall in GWP (Rehdanz and Maddison 2005) for a 1°C rise – were published in papers written before 1°C warming had occurred. So how did economists generate these numbers? The answer is shockingly simple: *they made them up.*

They used two main methods to generate pseudo-data on global warming's effect on the economy. Firstly, they acted *as if* climate change was merely a change in the weather, so that anything done indoors or underground would be 'negligibly affected by climate change' (Nordhaus 1991c, p. 930). The IPCC spouted the same assumption two decades later:

FAQ 10.3 | Are other economic sectors vulnerable to climate change too?

Economic activities such as agriculture, forestry, fisheries, and mining are exposed to the weather and thus vulnerable to climate change. *Other economic activities, such as manufacturing and services, largely take place in controlled environments and are not really exposed to climate change.* (Arent et al. 2014, p. 688, emphasis added)

They then added up damages expected from temperature increases for industries that necessarily occur outdoors – farming, forestry, construction, and so on – and called these 'enumerated' damages. They assumed damages to the rest of the economy would be zero (see table 4.1). In other words, Nordhaus assumed that anything done under a roof would be unaffected by climate change, so that a mere 13 per cent of the economy would be affected by it. The same assumption has been made by all other Neoclassical economists working on climate change.

Secondly, they acted *as if* existing data on the relatively weak relationship between temperature today and income today could be used 'as an analogue for climate change' (Maddison and Rehdanz 2011, p. 2438). To quote Richard

Table 4.1. Extract from Nordhaus's table 5: breakdown of economic activity by vulnerability to climatic change in 1991 US$ terms (Nordhaus 1991c, Table 5, p. 931)

Sector	Percentage of total
Negligible effect	
Manufacturing and mining	26.0
Other transportation and communication	5.5
Finance, insurance, and balance real estate	11.4
Trade and other services	27.9
Government services	14.0
Rest of world	2.1
Total 'negligible effect'	86.9

Tol, who was one of two lead co-authors of the Economics chapter of the IPCC Report in 2014, this approach:

> is based on direct estimates of the welfare impacts, *using observed variations (across space within a single country) in prices and expenditures to discern the effect of climate. **Mendelsohn assumes that the observed variation of economic activity with climate over space holds over time as well;** and uses climate models to estimate the future effect of climate change.* (Tol 2009, p. 32, emphasis added)

These economists measured the statistical relationship between temperature and income today, and used parameters derived from that relationship to estimate the damages from global warming. Since climate today is a relatively unimportant factor in income today – in that areas with vastly different temperatures today can have very similar incomes – this portrays increasing global temperatures as a relatively trivial phenomenon, in stark contrast to the guidance of scientists noted above.

If the absurdity of these two methods isn't immediately obvious to you, contrast these assumptions to the predictions of scientists about the impact of global warming on the frequency of deadly combinations of heat and humidity.

According to Mora and colleagues, a 5.5°C increase in global temperatures would mean that 'mid-latitudes (for example, 40° N or S) will be exposed to 60 deadly days per year' (Mora et al. 2017, p. 504). *Even if* factories and shops were not burnt down or flooded in these regions, you would be unlikely to be able to find workers to work in them, because anyone sensible would have left these uninhabitable regions of the planet – which are home to 74 per cent of humans today.

The second assumption means that, if two places today are similar, except for their average temperature, then the economic future of the colder place (say, Maryland) under global warming can be estimated by comparing it with the economy of a warmer place today (say, Florida). Richard

Tol made precisely this claim in a discussion on Twitter in June 2019:

> *Tol*: 10K[11] is less than the temperature distance between Alaska and Maryland (about equally rich), or between Iowa and Florida (about equally rich). Climate is not a primary driver of income.
>
> *Daniel Swain*: A global climate 10 degrees warmer than present is not remotely the same thing as taking the current climate and simply adding 10 degrees everywhere. This is an admittedly widespread misconception, but arguably quite a dangerous one.
>
> *Tol*: That's not the point, Daniel. We observe that people thrive in very different climates, and that some thrive and others do not in the same climate. Climate determinism therefore has no empirical support.
>
> And if a relationship does not hold for climate variations over space, you cannot confidently assert that it holds over time.

Maryland's average temperature between 1971 and 2000 was 12.3°C, and Florida's was 21.5°C – so there is roughly a 10°C difference between them today. Maryland's per capita income in 2000 was about $33,000, and Florida's was $26,000, so Maryland's income was about 20 per cent higher than Florida's. Therefore, 'making use of spatial variations in the existing climate as an analogue for climate change' (Maddison and Rehdanz 2011, p. 2438) implies that 10°C of global warming would reduce Maryland's average income by about 20 per cent.

This is absurd. According to scientists, even a 5.5°C increase in global temperature would render Maryland uninhabitable. At that temperature level, New York – which is about 250 kilometres north of Maryland – would experience 55 days of deadly heat and humidity per year. The impact of another 4°C or more of warming, as in this example, is simply unthinkable. *You simply cannot use comparative temperature and income data today as a proxy for climate change.* If you drive from Maryland to

Florida today, the ambient temperature will rise by about 10°C, but there will be no change in the global climate: the Arctic will be covered in ice when you leave Maryland, and it will still be covered in ice when you arrive in Miami. But if global temperatures rise by even 5.5°C, then according to scientists (Mora et al. 2017; Steffen et al. 2018), the Arctic will go from being covered in ice today, to having an average temperature of more than 22°C, and Greenland and Antarctica will be rapidly heading towards being ice-free. The parts of Maryland that were still above sea level in such a world would be an inhospitable desert, and any humans foolish enough to have remained there would have died of heat stroke.

If these two assumptions by economists were defensible, then so too would be their predictions that climate change will be, to quote one of the economist-respondents to Nordhaus's survey in 1994, 'small potatoes' (Nordhaus 1994, p. 48). But if they are false – which they manifestly are – then predictions like Nordhaus's of 'damage of 2.0 percent of income at 3°C, and 7.9 percent of global income at a global temperature rise of 6°C' (Nordhaus 2018b, p. 345) will be wildly wrong. We will find ourselves in a climate that will cause catastrophic damages to our economic and social systems. Climate change will make the devastation wrought by Covid-19 look like a picnic.

With global warming to date having pushed global average temperatures to 1.3°C above the average for 1900–20,[12] we are fast approaching the point where reality will let us discern who is right: Neoclassical economists, or climate scientists, whom Nordhaus himself noted expected damages '20 to 30 times higher than mainstream economists' (Nordhaus 1994, p. 49). I have no doubt that the scientists will prove far closer to the mark than the economists.

Neoclassical climate change economics will therefore prove to be an even worse predictor of the near future of the climate than the Neoclassical macroeconomics was of the near future of the macroeconomy in 2007. But, unlike their failure to see the GFC coming, this will not be an error that is relatively easily attenuated by sensible (non-Neoclassical!) economic policy. Civilization will instead be in a fight for its survival.

Economists may well escape scrutiny on this greatest of failures, simply because reacting to the consequences of climate change may leave us with no time to bring to account those who fooled us – and themselves – into not taking the threat seriously enough. There are also many other parties who can be accused of trivializing the dangers of climate change, from fossil fuel corporations to professional 'climate change sceptics' like Bjorn Lomborg (Lomborg 2020). Maybe economists will escape attention in the melee.

But if these economists are called to task for their appallingly bad work (Keen 2020a), one issue will be to what extent their failure was due to their own personal foibles, and to what extent it was due to the nature of mainstream economics itself.

The blame for Nordhaus's blatant misrepresentation of the scientific literature on tipping elements in the climate is something that can be laid only at Nordhaus's feet: nothing in Neoclassical economics forced him to so utterly misrepresent Lenton's findings (Lenton et al. 2008).

But the fact that referees for economics journals recommended publication of papers which assumed that 87 per cent of industry would be unaffected by climate change because it happens in 'carefully controlled environments' (Nordhaus 1991c, p. 930), and which treated the geographic relationship between temperature and income as a proxy for the relationship between global warming and income (Mendelsohn et al. 2000), points to a deep pathology in economics itself that I call 'the Neoclassical disease'. This is the practice of treating assumptions whose truth is critical to the relevance of the theory as mere 'simplifying assumptions', and not subjecting them to serious scrutiny.

5

The Neoclassical disease

I was presenting my model of Minsky's 'Financial Instability Hypothesis' at the Western Economic Association conference in 2011 – which took 'Western' to extremes by being held in Brisbane, Australia – when a young American member of the audience became visibly agitated. I had earlier attended his session, where he had enthusiastically presented his own 'rational expectations' macroeconomic model. An essential component of the Neoclassical definition of 'rational expectations' is that 'rational' people have a model of the economy – a Neoclassical one, of course! – which enables them to accurately predict the future, and which also renders government policy ineffective:

> expectations, since they are informed predictions of future events, are essentially the same as the predictions of the relevant economic theory. (Muth 1961, p. 316) ... by virtue of the assumption that expectations are rational, there is no feedback rule that the authority can employ and expect to be able systematically to fool the public. (Sargent and Wallace 1976, p. 182)

This is not how the dictionary defines 'rational': it's closer to the dictionary definition of 'prophetic'. Anyone who accepts the Neoclassical definition of 'rational' has, to some significant degree, lost touch with reality. So, I was expecting an 'irrational' reaction from this young zealot to my talk.

And Bingo! Unable to restrain himself, he blurted out 'But, but you're assuming people are *idiots*!' in the middle of my talk. I then asked him 'well, did you predict the Great Recession?', to which he replied, rather querulously, 'Um, no'. I then said 'So by your own definition, you're an idiot. Why shouldn't I model the world as being made up of people like you?'

He tried to engage me in further debate after the session, and shouted 'But we have to make some simplifying assumptions!' at me as I left the seminar room. My riposte, cast over my receding shoulder, was 'Mate, you have to learn the difference between a simplifying assumption and a fantasy'.

That, in essence, is the Neoclassical disease: treating something that any outside observer would regard as a fantasy as a 'simplifying assumption', and asserting that the fantasy cannot be questioned when one challenges the resulting model. Economics abounds in such fantastical assumptions because of the problem outlined in the first chapter: economics has, time and time again, been subject to paradigm-challenging anomalies, but rather than accepting the challenge, economists have responded by making ridiculous assumptions to shield the paradigm from criticism.

There are an abundance of examples, but the most apposite here is the Neoclassical reaction to empirical research in the 1940s by Richard Lester (Lester 1946) into the actual cost structure of firms. This study had many precursors (Garver et al. 1938; Hall and Hitch 1939; Means 1935, 1936; Tucker 1937, 1938), *all* of which discovered the same phenomenon: whereas economic theory assumed marginal costs (the additional costs incurred to produce the last unit of output) rose as output rose, empirical research found that actual firms had constant or falling marginal costs, right out to full capacity output. This made researchers like Lester very impatient with the textbook model of firms:

> The conventional explanation of the output and employment policies of individual firms runs in terms of maximizing profits by equating marginal revenue and marginal cost. Student protests that their entrepreneurial parents claim not to operate on the marginal principle have apparently failed to shake the confidence of the textbook writers in the validity of the marginal analysis. (Lester 1946, p. 63)

The finding that actual firms have constant or falling marginal costs is a critical challenge to the Neoclassical theory of the firm because, if so, then there is no 'supply curve'. As Mankiw's textbook states emphatically, '*The competitive firm's short-run supply curve is the portion of its marginal-cost curve that lies above average variable cost*' (Mankiw 2001, p. 298) and '*The competitive firm's long-run supply curve is the portion of its marginal cost curve that lies above average total cost*' (Mankiw 2001, p. 301).

If marginal cost – the cost of producing the last unit made – is constant or falling, then there is no 'portion of its marginal-cost curve that lies above average variable cost': marginal cost is either equal to average variable cost (if marginal cost is constant) or below it (if it is falling). A constant or falling marginal cost curve will also always be lower than average total costs (the sum of fixed and variable costs, divided by the number of units produced), so that any firm that set price equal to marginal cost – a fundamental condition in the Neoclassical model of 'perfect competition' – would lose money. Since most firms have constant or falling marginal cost, as empirical studies before and after Lester (Blinder 1998; Downward 1994; Eiteman 1947; Eiteman and Guthrie 1952; Hall 1988; Means 1972) have confirmed, then the Neoclassical theory of price being set by the intersection of supply and demand schedules can't possibly be correct.

From a realist perspective, this is hardly amazing. The Neoclassical model of production is simply an anagram of its model of consumer behaviour, where consumers gain utility by consuming a range of commodities that are easily substituted for each other. Each new unit of a commodity consumed adds to total utility, but at a declining rate – hence the concept of 'diminishing marginal utility'. Similarly, the model of production has a factory that can take a range of easily substitutable inputs and convert them into outputs, but these variable inputs are applied to a constant amount of fixed capital – a bit like food into the consumer's belly, where the quantity and composition of inputs are highly variable, while the stomach is a fixed size (at least in the 'short run'). Each input has positive 'marginal productivity' – each new unit of input adds to total output – but at a falling rate, hence 'diminishing marginal productivity'. This in turn causes rising marginal cost: each additional unit of a variable input costs the same amount to buy, but produces less output, so marginal cost rises.

In the real world, factories are nothing like a consumer's stomach. They are instead designed by engineers to achieve maximum efficiency at full capacity, but they also necessarily start with unused capacity – otherwise the factory would be too small to accommodate growth in demand over time. As demand grows, new machines are added (or machinery which was idle is turned on) and paired with new variable inputs (labour and raw materials) so that per-machine productivity remains constant, while the overall efficiency of the factory rises as it approaches full capacity. Consequently, so long as it can price its output above its average cost of production, the more units sold, the more profit is made, and the ideal output level is 100 per cent of capacity (long before this point is reached, the firm should be building a new factory with even lower costs). This is what Sraffa hypothesized on logical grounds in 1926 (Sraffa 1926), and what Lester reported in his 1946 survey:

Individual-firm studies ... indicate that average variable costs (and marginal costs) tend to be constant per unit of product over the usual range of output, which includes up to practically full capacity ... In reply to the question, 'At what level of operations are your profits generally greatest under peacetime conditions?' 42 firms answered 100 per cent of plant capacity. The remaining 11 replies ranged from 75 to 95 per cent of capacity. (Lester 1946, pp. 67–8)

A realism-oriented discipline would have taken this empirical contradiction of its original model to heart, and come up with a new model of how prices are set which is compatible with constant or falling marginal costs – such as Kalecki's 'degree of monopoly' markup-pricing model, for example (Kalecki 1942; Kriesler 1988). But instead, the main economic response to this paper was Milton Friedman's infamous 'assumptions don't matter' methodology paper (Friedman 1953), in which Friedman advised economists to not even bother to read Lester's research:

The lengthy discussion on marginal analysis in the *American Economic Review* some years ago is an even clearer, though much less important, example. The articles on both sides of the controversy largely neglect what seems to me clearly the main issue – the conformity to experience of the implications of the marginal analysis – and concentrate on the largely irrelevant question whether businessmen do or do not in fact reach their decisions by consulting schedules, or curves, or multivariable functions showing marginal cost and marginal revenue. (Friedman 1953, p. 15)

In place of accepting that empirical data contradicted Neoclassical theory, Friedman recommended an '*as if*' approach: even though we know firms don't behave as our model suggests, let's model them 'as if' they do:

It is only a short step from these examples to the economic hypothesis that under a wide range of circumstances individual firms behave *as if* they were seeking rationally to maximize their expected returns ... and had full knowledge of the data needed to succeed in this attempt; *as if*, that is, they knew the relevant cost and demand functions, calculated marginal cost and marginal revenue from all actions open to them, and pushed each line of action to the point at which the relevant marginal cost and marginal revenue were equal. (Friedman 2007, p. 158)

However, Lester's research was not about whether or not businesses actually used calculus to determine the profit-maximizing level of output, but whether the conditions needed for that method to work in the first place actually applied in the real world. He, like every researcher on this topic before and after him, found that they did not. 'Diminishing marginal productivity' did not apply to actual production processes, marginal cost was either constant or fell as output increased, and average costs fell all the way out to capacity. Hence, so long as price exceeded average cost, the sensible strategy was to sell as many units as possible. But Neoclassical economists didn't want to hear this message, and Friedman's 'as if' methodology let them ignore it – as they have done ever since (Blinder 1998).[1]

As well as successfully suppressing the attention paid to empirical research into firms, Friedman also provided a convenient argument that economists could use against *any* criticism of any of their models on the grounds of that their assumptions were unrealistic. In what became known as the 'F-twist', Friedman argued that *unrealistic assumptions were indicative of a good theory*, rather than a bad one:

the relation between the significance of a theory and the 'realism' of its 'assumptions' is almost the opposite of that suggested by the view under criticism. Truly important and significant hypotheses will be found to have 'assumptions' that are wildly inaccurate descriptive representations of reality, and, in general, *the more significant the theory, the more unrealistic the assumptions* (in this sense) ...

To put this point less paradoxically, the relevant question to ask about the 'assumptions' of a theory is not whether they are descriptively 'realistic,' for they never are, but whether they are sufficiently good approximations for the purpose in hand. And this question can be answered only by seeing whether the theory works, which means whether it yields sufficiently accurate predictions. The two supposedly independent tests thus reduce to one test. (Friedman 2007, p. 153, emphasis added)

This is spin disguised as methodology. For a start, as philosopher Alan Musgrave pointed out brilliantly (Musgrave 1981), Friedman's 'the more significant the theory, the more unrealistic the assumptions' argument is only even passably true of the simplest class of assumption, which Musgrave labels, for obvious reasons, 'simplifying assumptions'. This is the decision to leave out some obvious aspect of reality, in the context of an experiment where you expect that aspect to play a minor role. Air resistance when heavy objects are dropped from a building is a good example. When Galileo experimentally contradicted the belief of the prevailing Aristotelian paradigm that heavy objects fell faster than light objects, he effectively ignored the impact of air resistance. If he had taken it into account, he would have had to construct a vastly more complicated apparatus, but the effect on the experiment would have been slight, and the results would still have contradicted the Aristotelian paradigm.

However, Friedman's argument is utterly false when it is applied to another class of assumptions, which Musgrave labels 'domain assumptions'. These are assumptions that delineate the boundaries within which the theory to be tested actually applies. If the assumption holds, then so will the theory. If the assumption is false, then so will be the theory. In the case of domain assumptions therefore, it is vitally necessary to know whether they hold or not: you can't simply take such an assumption for granted.

For examples of domain assumptions, you need look no further than *the assumptions that Neoclassical economists make all the damn time* that are manifestly false, but which if they were true, then the resulting theory would also be true. From the cornucopia of riches of such assumptions, possibly the most absurd of all relate to the mental gymnastics Neoclassical economists have undertaken to avoid the implications of the 'Sonnenschein–Mantel–Debreu' theorem (as discussed in chapter 3). Gorman's assumption, reproduced on page 96 and below, is bad enough. But it pales into insignificance in comparison to the one Samuelson used to justify this confident statement in his undergraduate textbook (written jointly with William Nordhaus):

> The market demand curve is found by adding together the quantities demanded by all individuals at each price. *Does the market demand curve obey the law of downward-sloping demand? It certainly does.* (Samuelson and Nordhaus 2010b, p. 48, emphasis added)

I knew that this statement was false when I first read it. The only mystery to me was whether Samuelson and Nordhaus were simply bullshitting – *yes I know this is an academic book, but what else can you call what Neoclassical economists routinely do?* – or whether they thought they had proven otherwise. It turned out to be the latter. In a paper entitled 'Social Indifference Curves' (Samuelson 1956), Samuelson confronted the same dilemma that Gorman considered three years earlier. Neoclassical theory easily derives the 'Law of Demand' for one individual: the statement that if a good gets more expensive, a given consumer will buy less of it. Make apples more expensive relative to oranges, and the consumer will buy fewer apples.

But that proof for the individual assumes that changing prices does not change the individual's income. You can't assume that when you attempt to construct a market demand curve for a specific economy. While one individual's income might not be altered when you make apples relatively more expensive than oranges, when you consider the entire economy – as you must to construct a market demand curve – then you are going to make apple producers wealthier and orange producers poorer. If they also have different tastes, then the change in income distribution caused by the change in relative prices will affect demand in turn, and in possibly perverse ways. For example, apple producers might regard vodka and apple juice as a luxury, while orange producers might prefer Tequila Sunrises. Then quite possibly, making apples more expensive might increase the demand for apples, because the now-wealthier apple producers (and producers of other goods whose incomes also rise) buy more apples.

The only way to avoid this outcome is a patently absurd assumption, which Samuelson properly points out is an 'impossibility theorem':

> The common sense of this impossibility theorem is easy to grasp. Allocating the same totals differently among people must generally change the resulting equilibrium price ratio. The only exception is where tastes are identical, not only for all men, but also for all men when they are rich or poor. (Samuelson 1956, p. 5)

So far, so good: Samuelson is describing as absurd the assumption that Gorman described as 'intuitively reasonable' three years earlier, that 'an extra unit of purchasing power should be spent in the same way no matter to whom it is given' (Gorman 1953, p. 64). But then, he imagines that a 'family indifference curve' can be constructed, because:

> since blood is thicker than water, the preferences of the different members are interrelated by what might be called a 'consensus' or 'social welfare function' which takes into account the deservingness or ethical worths of the consumption levels of each of the members. The family acts as if it were maximizing their [sic] joint welfare function. (Samuelson 1956, p. 10)

Notice the 'as if' in the final sentence: 'The family acts *as if* it were maximizing their joint welfare function'. So, the typical American family is one big, happy unit, which pools all family income and then shares it out so that everyone is OK with the distribution of income, before any shopping takes place? Not from what I can see in both fact and fiction on conventional and social media! But OK, Samuelson has moved from individuals to families with only a moderately outrageous assumption, of using a harmonious family as his model rather than a fractious one.

But then came the *coup de grâce*: how do we get from a harmonious family to the whole of society? Simple! *We assume that all of society operates like one big, happy family*:

> The same argument will apply to all of society *if optimal reallocations of income can be assumed to keep the ethical worth of each person's marginal dollar equal.* (Samuelson 1956, p. 21, emphasis added)

Oh please! The United States of America, home to a libertarian philosophy exalting 'freedom' above all else, championing the absence of centralized control, divided by politics, class and race, with by far the highest murder and incarceration rates in the developed world, has sitting over it some political process – *a benevolent central authority perhaps* – that reallocates income so that everybody is happy about its distribution, before any buying and selling takes place?

Before you think I'm merely being sarcastic here, this is how the leading PhD-level Neoclassical textbook *Microeconomics* (Mas-Colell et al. 1995) puts Samuelson's assumption *approvingly*:

> Let us now hypothesize that there is a process, *a benevolent central authority perhaps*, that, for any given prices p and aggregate wealth function w, *redistributes wealth in order to maximize social welfare.* (Mas-Colell et al. 1995, p. 117, emphasis added)

To me, the fact that Neoclassical economists are willing to accept a 'hypothesis' like this to maintain their paradigm is the strongest possible sign that it has failed, and is only kept alive by what John Quiggin characterized as zombie thinking (Quiggin 2010). Here is the dominant, mainstream model of 'free market' capitalism, willingly assuming the existence of a 'benevolent central authority' as an integral part of a 'free market'.

The madness of this assumption aside, if there was a planet on which such a 'free market' was overseen by such a 'benevolent central authority', it would be possible to explain downward-sloping market demand curves using Neoclassical economic theory. But are we on that planet? No: on this one, Americans can't even agree on the tallying of votes in an election. *Therefore, because the assumption is false, so is the theory.* It is a domain assumption, not a simplifying assumption.

But Samuelson's paper was approved for publication by referees. The same is done, time and time again, when the choice is between realism and preserving Neoclassical economic beliefs: reality loses out. Friedman's paper simply codified a common practice in economics: using patently false domain assumptions to paper over profound logical problems in the underlying theory.

In the context of this ingrained dishonesty in how Neoclassical economics has developed, an assumption like Nordhaus's that, of America's total GDP, 87 per cent is created 'in sectors that are negligibly affected by climate change' (Nordhaus 1991c, p. 930), is water off a duck's back for referees who already accept such things as 'perfect foresight' as a legitimate assumption in an economic model (Debreu 1959).[2] So rather than being rejected by referees, the insane proposition that a roof will protect you from climate change is treated as a 'simplifying assumption', and accepted.

Equally probably, they are, like Nordhaus himself, innately climate change trivializers: 'Climate change is likely to produce a combination of gains and losses with no strong presumption of substantial net economic damages' (Nordhaus 1991c, p. 933); 'I am known to the respondents as one who has developed estimates of the impact of climatic change that are modest compared with some of the scientific concerns and popular rhetoric' (Nordhaus 1994, p. 46). They could actually agree with Nordhaus's false assumption, and let it pass for that reason. As with the Global Financial Crisis in 2007, mainstream economists will be amongst those who will be most surprised by the coming ecological crisis.

The only remaining defence of Friedman's 'don't judge a theory by its assumptions' methodology is that doing so is a subjective judgement, relying on the opinions of referees, whereas Friedman's test of waiting to see whether the theory 'yields sufficiently accurate predictions' (Friedman 2007, p. 153) is objective, relying on the results of the experiment in the real world. In effect, this argues in favour of a weak publication standard, of admitting almost any assumption, and letting reality decide whether the theory is a good description of reality instead.

However, as the vignette at the start of this chapter illustrates, this tolerant treatment of assumptions by Neoclassicals is applied only to assumptions that fit into, or preserve, the Neoclassical paradigm. When you make assumptions that are incompatible with Neoclassical economics, your papers are rejected out of hand *because* of its assumptions – and often by editors using Neoclassical assumptions to justify doing so (Keen 2013a).[3]

Critically in the case of the economics of climate change, this free pass for bad methodology is only justifiable if the issue being considered has no significant and irreversible ramifications. If you have a crazy theory about consumer behaviour, and you test it in an experiment and it fails, then the only victims are the experimental subjects, and the theory improves as the results of the failure are incorporated into it.

But if your theory is about the impact of climate change on the future of human civilization? Then if your assumption is false, the consequences for human civilization are catastrophic and irreversible. There is no 'Planet B'. Treating assumptions this way in the context of climate change 'amounts to conducting a one-time, irreversible experiment of unknown outcome with the habitability of the entire planet' (DeCanio 2003, p. 3). We simply cannot afford the consequences of these assumptions being wrong – as they manifestly are.

However, because Friedman's methodology is widely accepted by Neoclassical economists, and taught in economics textbooks (Mankiw 2012, pp. 22–4), Neoclassical referees let Nordhaus's crazy assumption pass.

Then the mechanics of the refereeing process took over, and amplified the problem. Given the tiny number of papers published in economics journals on climate change – Nicholas Stern observed that 'the *Quarterly Journal of Economics*, which is currently the most-cited journal in the field of economics, has never published an article on climate change', while the top nine general economics journals have published just fifty-seven papers, out of a total of over 77,000 (Oswald and Stern 2019) – Nordhaus would already have been a 'go to' referee on climate change papers for editors of economics journals, after the publication of 'Measurement without Data' – his attack on the precursor to the *Limits to Growth* model in 1973 (Nordhaus 1973) – and his subsequent papers on energy and climate issues (National Research Council 1978; Nordhaus et al. 1973, 1974a, 1974b, 1976, 1977, 1980a, 1980b, 1982, 1986, 1991a, 1991b). This would have enabled him to enforce a degree of conformity in papers on the economics of climate change, which would then have resulted in more referees who concurred with Nordhaus's position, further enforcing a trivializing hegemony on academic publications on the economics of climate change.

Richard Tol himself observed that the researchers in this field are tightly connected: 'Nordhaus and Mendelsohn are colleagues and collaborators at Yale University; at University College of London, Fankhauser, Maddison, and I all worked with David Pearce and one another, while Rehdanz was a student of Maddison and mine' (Tol 2009, p. 31). A refereeing process calling upon such a limited pool of researchers as referees could, as even Tol deduced, lead to groupthink:

> it is quite possible that the estimates are not independent, as there are only a relatively small number of studies, based on similar data, by authors who know each other well ... although the number of researchers who published marginal damage cost estimates is larger than the number of researchers who published total impact estimates, it is still a reasonably small and close-knit community who may be subject to group-think, peer pressure, and self-censoring. (Tol 2009, pp. 37, 42–3)

The refereeing process in economics journals thus enforces the hegemony of Neoclassical economics in general, while in climate change, it has entrenched a denialist perspective for almost fifty years – ever since William Nordhaus destroyed the credibility of a rival methodology to Neoclassical economics known as 'system dynamics'. It is more than a little ironic that, given the cavalier attitude that Nordhaus has since displayed towards data on climate change, his attack focused on Forrester's treatment of data (Nordhaus 1973).

Nordhaus's successful – and manifestly fallacious (Forrester et al. 1974) – dismissal of system dynamics in 'Measurement without Data' has had disastrous consequences. First and foremost, he replaced the prescient warnings of the original *Limits to Growth* study (Meadows et al. 1972; Turner 2008, 2014) with his own Panglossian belief in the capacity for effectively unlimited growth on a finite planet. Had policymakers taken *Limits to Growth* seriously, we might well have begun the gradual implementation of the policies they recommended to avoid a calamitous future. Instead, meaningful action on climate change was delayed by half a century, over which time humanity's pressure on the biosphere has more than trebled. Significant, highly damaging climate change is now a certainty, and the actions needed to address it will be far more drastic than the methods which could have been employed fifty years ago.

Secondly, system dynamics was in fact the solution that Jevons, one of the founding fathers of Neoclassical economics, longed for eighty years earlier: a method by which the manifestly inadequate reliance upon equilibrium modelling could be replaced by dynamics 'in all its natural complexity':

> We must carefully distinguish, at the same time, between the Statics and Dynamics of this subject. The real condition of industry is one of perpetual motion and change. Commodities are being continually manufactured and exchanged and consumed. *If we wished to have a complete solution of the problem in all its natural complexity, we should have to treat it as a problem of motion – a problem of dynamics.* But it would surely be absurd to attempt the more difficult question when the more easy one is yet so imperfectly within our power. It is only as a purely statical problem that I can venture to treat the action of exchange. (Jevons 1888, p. 93, emphasis added)

This crucial methodological error by economists must be reversed. System dynamics can and should be the methodological core of a new economics, which will have to be built by students of economics over the objections – and behind the backs – of their Neoclassical instructors.

6
Conclusion: Be the change

Looking back on the fifty years since I first became aware of its flaws, the word that summarizes my feelings about Neoclassical economics today is that it is, as Marx once described the proto-Neoclassical Jean-Baptiste Say, 'dull' (Marx 1857 [1993], footnote pp. 267–8). Its vision of capitalism at its best is a system manifesting the harmony of equilibrium, where everyone is paid their just return (their 'marginal product'), growth is occurring smoothly at a rate that maximizes social utility through time, and everyone is motivated by consumption – rather than accumulation and power – because, to quote Say, 'the producers, though they have all of them the air of demanding money for their goods, do in reality demand merchandise for their merchandise' (Say 1821, Chapter 18).

What a bland picture of the complex, changing world in which we live!

For all its flaws, capitalism was and remains an exciting social system. For all *his* flaws (Keen 1993a, 1993b), Marx put this best, in his own *Manifesto*. Though it called for the overthrow of capitalism, *The Communist Manifesto* was also a paean to the creative and transformative nature of capitalism and its distinctive class, whom Marx called 'the bourgeoisie', and we might today call 'entrepreneurs'. For them, the guiding principle is not 'merchandise for their merchandise', said Marx, but 'Accumulate, accumulate! That is Moses and the prophets!' (Marx 1867, Chapter 24). In contrast to the staid conservatism of the dominant classes of previous social systems, Marx declared that 'the bourgeoisie cannot exist without constantly revolutionizing the instruments of production, and thereby the relations of production, and with them the whole relations of society':

> Conservation of the old modes of production in unaltered form, was, on the contrary, the first condition of existence for all earlier industrial classes. *Constant revolutionizing of production, uninterrupted disturbance of all social conditions, everlasting uncertainty and agitation distinguish the bourgeois epoch from all earlier ones.* All fixed, fast frozen relations, with their train of ancient and venerable prejudices and opinions, are swept away, all new-formed ones become antiquated before they can ossify. All that is solid melts into air, all that is holy is profaned, and man is at last compelled to face with sober senses his real condition of life and his relations with his kind. (Marx and Engels 1848 [2017], p. 54, emphasis added)

How did Marx's exciting portrayal of capitalism lose out to Say's vapid vision?

In part, this was deliberate. Nitzan and Bichler point out that the quintessential nineteenth-century robber-baron John D. Rockefeller regarded his $45 million endowment to the Baptist University of Chicago, which would eventually become the intellectual home of Milton Friedman, as 'the best investment I ever made' (Nitzan and Bichler 2009, p. 76). As De Vroey argued, 'the new paradigm was especially attractive because it looked as scientific as the natural sciences theories, while it eluded the dangerous topics of class interests and transformation of the system ... This inoffensiveness was and is, from the viewpoint of the capitalist ruling class, the main quality of the neoclassical paradigm' (De Vroey 1975, p. 435).

This explains the appeal of Neoclassical economics to establishment interests, but it doesn't explain its appeal to Neoclassical economists themselves. There, I believe, the vision of capitalism as a utopia is what excites the Neoclassical mind – and this utopia only applies in equilibrium, whether that be the Partial equilibrium of Marshall, the General equilibrium of Walras, the Nash equilibrium of game theory, or Ramsey's (Ramsey 1928) inter-temporal equilibrium that is the foundation of Real Business Cycle and Dynamic Stochastic General Equilibrium models. This reliance upon equilibrium as a foundation for the welfare claims of Neoclassical economics turned the reluctant use of equilibrium techniques by the founders of Neoclassical economics – as the quote from Jevons in the previous chapter indicates – into a secular religion.

Looked at dispassionately, this is a religion which has proven that its God doesn't exist. Its many failures point in the direction that may, finally, lead to a passably scientific economics.

Neoclassical economics abolished the concept of social classes, let alone class conflict, by the mechanism of the marginal productivity theory of income distribution, and the classless construct of the 'representative agent'. But the Cambridge Controversies – where, it must be remembered, Samuelson conceded defeat (Samuelson 1966) – showed that the return to capital cannot be its marginal product (Garegnani 1970; Pasinetti 1969), while the Sonnenschein–Mantel–Debreu theorem (Sonnenschein 1972, 1973a, 1973b) implies, as Alan Kirman put it, that:

> demand and expenditure functions if they are to be set against reality must be defined at some reasonably high level of aggregation. The idea that we should start at the level of the isolated individual is one which we may well have to abandon. (Kirman 1989, p. 138)

These results validate the Classical school's approach of dividing society into social classes, and of treating profit as a residual, whose scale depends on the relative power of those social classes. Issues of power and the distribution of income, which were assumed away by Neoclassical economics, come back to centre stage.

Similarly, Neoclassical economics could only take the finance sector off the economic stage by using a manifestly false model of banking. Now that the reality that banks create money is acknowledged, so too must be the role of the finance sector in creating asset price bubbles (see figures 2.12 and 2.14) and financial crises (see figure 3.4), and in enabling the accumulation and concealment of wealth.

These necessary aspects of a realistic New Economics have a paradoxical political outcome. They result from having a fearless agnosticism about ideology and politics: to acknowledge that capitalism is a class system is simply acknowledging a fact, while the Neoclassical 'representative agent' is a fiction. But they also mean that economics is necessarily political. With a class-based analysis, the consequences for different social classes of different economic policies must be confronted. The distributions of income, wealth and power matter, and economists can no longer hide behind aggregate cost–benefit analysis when debating policy.

The New Economics must also be grounded in the actual dynamics, complexity and chaos of capitalism. Though there is nothing political about this – it is simply a case of using the tools of analysis that suit the dynamic, evolutionary system that capitalism itself is – I expect that this dynamic foundation will lead to an economics that will be as progressive as the equilibrium foundation of Neoclassical economics proved to be reactionary.

The preceding chapters have sketched out essential elements of a post-Neoclassical economic paradigm: the need for a monetary foundation, the need to understand complexity, the need to be grounded in the biophysics of production using energy and matter, to be integrated with a proper understanding of ecology, and above all, the need for realism in its assumptions and methods, as opposed to the Neoclassical reliance upon armchair fantasies. The question with which I close this book is: What should the mathematical foundation of this new paradigm be?

I am fully aware that some of my non-Neoclassical colleagues believe that we should eschew mathematical modelling completely (Lawson 2013). My rejoinders in Keen (2015a) were that Lawson's critique applies to linear models rather than nonlinear ones, and that mathematics has been abused, not used, by Neoclassicals. Failing to do mathematical modelling cedes to the Neoclassicals a vital space for the formation of economic thought, economic policy and the shaping of society, both in practice, and in people's mental image of the economy.

While mathematics has limitations in describing complex social systems, rather than ceding this tool to Neoclassical economists, we must instead supplant them. As Nordhaus and colleagues have ably demonstrated, Neoclassical economists have no qualms about providing the numerical estimates that politicians, bureaucrats and businessmen crave. Those numbers, fallacious or not, shape economic policy. The visual form in which their mathematics is portrayed, the ubiquitous totem of the intersecting supply and demand curves, is also the mental picture that the majority of people have of the economy, from the woman on the street to the politicians in parliament. We cannot afford to abrogate this territory: we will not displace the Neoclassical totem from people's minds without our own mathematical and visual alternatives.

My nomination for the mathematical foundation of a post-Neoclassical economics is system dynamics, which was invented by the brilliant engineer Jay Forrester in the mid to late 1950s. Forrester had previously played a major role in the design of mechanical control systems for naval radar and gun mounts during the Second World War. After the war, he was a lead developer of the world's first aircraft simulator, the first random access memory system for computers, and even the world's first computer animation (Forrester 1995). In 1956, he submitted a paper to his Faculty at the Massachusetts Institute of Technology, discussing his conclusions from a three-month-long study of economics. Entitled 'Dynamic Models of Economic Systems and Industrial Organizations' (Forrester 2003), the note covered what he perceived as the weaknesses of existing economic models, and outlined an alternative approach. Sadly, his criticisms of economics are even more relevant today than when he made them in 1956. They are worth citing at length here:

> One of the striking shortcomings of most economic models is their failure to reflect adequately the structural form of the regenerative loops that make up our economic system. The flows of money, materials, and information feed one another around closed re-entering paths ... The behavior of such loops (their tendency to amplify or dampen distur-bances, their natural frequency of oscillation, their ability to shift the phase or timing of events which feed into them) is determined by characteristics which are usually omitted from the models in the literature. ...
>
> Present models neglect to interrelate adequately the flows of goods, money, information, and labor ...
>
> Linear equations have usually been used to describe a system whose essential characteristic, I believe, arise from its non-linearities ...
>
> Models, suitable only for long-range prediction, are often used with short-term influences and fluctuations omitted. This is justifiable only if the system is sufficiently linear to permit superposition, an assumption which has not been justified or defended and which is probably untrue. Therefore, the long-range trends are probably very much a function of the short-range behavior of a system ...
>
> Many models are formulated in terms of systems of simultaneous algebraic equations. These impress me as particularly unsuited to the kind of behavior being studied ...
>
> The models and their symbolism and notation are often abstracted so far from physical and social reality that they

lull one into overlooking otherwise evident departures from the world of men, money, and materials ...

Preoccupation with the determination of numerical coefficients to two or three decimal places sometimes overshadows the meaning and significance of those coefficients, while the very structure of the model may be in doubt ...

Very often the model and its results are judged by the logic with which the model is developed out of its founding assumptions, whereas the failures probably lie in those assumptions. (Forrester 2003, pp. 331–5)

In addition to providing a devastatingly accurate critique of mainstream economics, Forrester also sketched out an alternative approach, free of the limitations of existing economic models (then and now!), by which the dynamic structure of an economy could be accurately described. He emphasized structural realism, the explicit treatment of time, and the use of nonlinear differential, rather than linear algebraic or difference, equations:

The greatest possible detailed attention should be given to the actual sequences of actions which take place in the system ... consumers do not purchase (as implied by most past models) from producers of goods. They buy from retailers, who buy from wholesale distributors, who draw goods from factory warehouses ... Such a distinction and stress on reality can have a first-order effect on the degree to which a model matches the real system in performance ...

Time delays and their causes are of paramount importance ...

When an economic model is built with the proper structure, we may find that much of the apparent volatility and irrationality now ascribed to human behavior will disappear ...

Almost every characteristic that one examines in the economic system is highly non-linear ... In a sufficiently non-linear system we should expect, until shown otherwise, that the short-term behavior may set the stage for the longer-term reactions ...

The behavior that we wish to describe in economic systems seems much better described by non-linear differential equations than by the algebraic equations and matrix operations which are so often used …

The incremental time intervals for which the variables of a model are solved step-by-step in time must be much shorter than often supposed … This solution interval is unrelated to the interval at which national statistics and economic indicators are measured. (Forrester 2003, pp. 337–45)

He provided a stylized drawing of the endogenous cycles generated by the time delays in an advertising campaign, inspired by consulting work he was doing at the time for General Electric. This consulting task led to the development, by his computer programmer colleague Richard Bennett, of the first 'system dynamics' program, called SIMPLE: 'Simulation of Industrial Management Problems with Lots of Equations' (Forrester 1995), in 1958. System dynamics was born, and the first flowchart-based programs (Stella, IThink, Vensim), with a visual approach to building models of real-world complex systems, were developed soon afterwards.

The fundamental element of a system dynamics model is the integral equation. This takes a differential equation like, for example, 'The rate of change of population equals Births minus Deaths' and restates it as 'Population equals the Initial Population plus the Integral of Births minus Deaths' (see figure 6.1). The reason for using integration rather than differentiation is that system dynamics models are simulated numerically, and numerical integration (calculating the area beneath a curve) is a much more stable process than numerical differentiation (calculating the slope of a curve).

A system dynamics model will have from several to thousands of interrelated stocks, each of which is a 'system state', and the value of one state will affect that of one or more others via feedback effects. One of the simplest models is the one we discussed in chapter 3,

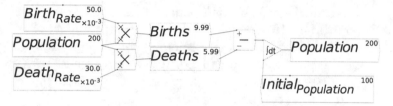

Figure 6.1. Simple population growth as an integral equation in *Minsky*. See http://www.profstevekeen.com/minsky/

the 'predator-prey' model, which has two system states – the number of predators and the number of prey – and the value of one affects the rate of change of the other. A model like World3, which was the basis of *Limits to Growth* (Meadows et al. 1972), has dozens of system states, and hundreds of feedback loops.

Today, system dynamics is commonplace in engineering and management, but it has never developed a strong following in economics. This is not despite the fact that it was first developed in response to shortcomings in economic modelling, but because of it. System dynamics was perceived as a fundamental challenge to the equilibrium-obsessed methodology of Neoclassical economics, and its challenge was effectively repulsed. The attack, in response to the application of this technology to issues of environmental economics – firstly by Forrester in the book *World Dynamics* (Forrester 1971, 1973), and then by Meadows, Meadows and Randers in *Limits to Growth* (Meadows et al. 1972) – was led by none other than William Nordhaus (Nordhaus 1973). You should appreciate the irony, given how Nordhaus has used obvious fallacies to make up his own numbers on climate change, that his main critique of Forrester's work was its poor attention to data.

Forrester's rebuttal of Nordhaus was in summary that 'each point made by Nordhaus rests on a misunderstanding of *World Dynamics*, a misuse of empirical data, or an inability to analyze properly the dynamic behavior of the model by static equilibrium methods' (Forrester et al. 1974, p. 169; Bardi 2018). Forrester was right and Nordhaus was wrong, but the damage was done. Though *Limits to Growth* had an enormous impact upon the public and the environmental movement, and its empirical predictions have held up well over time (Turner 2008, 2014), the technology itself was ridiculed out of contention in economics.

Consequently, while system dynamics technology has progressed enormously in engineering, outside the work of enthusiasts like Andresen, King, Radzicki, Tauheed and Wheat (Andresen 2018; King 2020; Radzicki 2003; Radzicki and Tauheed 2009; Wheat 2007, 2017) its application in even non-Neoclassical economics is almost non-existent. The engineering programs (like *Simulink*, Mathworks' extension to *Matlab*, and *System Modeler*, Wolfram's extension to *Mathematica*) are extremely powerful with modern interfaces, and are routinely used by engineers to model new technology before it is constructed, but they are tailored to the needs of engineers rather than economists. The management-social-science programs (like *Stella* and *Vensim*) have only a small user base compared to the engineering community, and their interfaces are very cumbersome and antiquated compared to modern software. In particular, the fact that connections between system states are made exclusively using 'wires' (like those shown in figure 6.1), while the equations are buried behind text boxes, results in 'spaghetti diagrams' that can be unintelligible to a non-professional audience.

Minsky is intended to address the deficiencies of existing programs for economic modelling, and to overcome their user interface shortcomings as well.

Minsky allows values to be 'passed by variable' as well as 'passed by wire' to reduce diagram clutter, equations are immediately visible on the design canvas (as illustrated by figure 6.1), and most importantly, it adds the unique feature of 'Godley Tables' that make it far easier to model financial flows. It is still a very 'young' program (at the time of writing, less than $500,000 has been spent on its development), but it is capable of simulating any deterministic dynamic model at present, and (if we can secure continued funding) we'll add more capabilities over time.[1]

My criticisms of existing software aside, the system dynamics community is vibrant and growing, with excellent online resources such as those provided by the System Dynamics Society, including over fifty online courses. There are a limited number of degree programs in system dynamics (see https://systemdynamics.org/courses/), but you can also teach yourself using the resources provided by the community. Donella Meadows' *Thinking in Systems* (Meadows 2008) is an excellent overview for the interested reader and intending practitioner alike. Melanie Mitchell's *Complexity: A Guided Tour* (Mitchell 2009) is a useful companion on the general issue of complex systems, and Hartmut Bossel's *Modeling and Simulation* (Bossel 1994) is a classic for intending practitioners. The pure and applied mathematics behind system dynamics is covered comprehensively and engagingly in Martin Braun's *Differential Equations and Their Applications* (Braun 1993).

Multi-agent-modelling (MAM) is also a useful technique for non-equilibrium modelling. I have supervised two excellent MAM PhD theses (Feher 2019; Gooding 2019), and there are some issues in economics – such as stock market dynamics, the evolution of pricing or the process of innovation – where evolutionary MAM is the only way to go. However, the overhead, in terms of programming skills, the difficulties in specifying and testing a model, and in evaluating its results, is enormous. This results in MAM projects often taking an order of magnitude longer to develop than their developers expect, and two orders of magnitude longer than a comparable system dynamics model. So, for reasons of parsimony, I recommend system dynamics first, and MAM only for tasks which system dynamics cannot undertake.

If you wish to delve deeper and actually contribute to a new, complex-systems-aware economics, then you have a daunting but rewarding task of contrarian education in economics ahead of you. I focus here on learning economics suitable for complex systems modelling, rather than the broad sweep of the history of economic thought, which you should also attempt to master.

6.1 Your contrarian education in economics

Outside of a handful of universities that, for reasons given in chapter 1, have a viable heterodox-friendly economics curriculum, you are not going to learn the economics you need to know in a formal university degree. The exceptions here include Leeds, Greenwich, SOAS and West England in the UK, UMKC, Utah and Stony Brook in the United States, and those in Europe associated with the EPOG program (see also the list of feasible courses at *The Mint* site https://yrpri.org/group/3990 and the Heterodox News site http://heterodoxnews.com/hed/study-programs.html). But, if you do your degree at a top-ranked university – and I fully understand the appeal of studying at a Cambridge or a Yale over, say, a Kingston – then you are going to have to undertake this part of your education on your own (however, if you find a rebel economist on staff at your Ivy League alma mater, introduce yourself and learn from – and support – him or her).

On the positive side, today's critical books and online resources provide a far richer coverage of critiques of the mainstream and alternative approaches to economics than was available in the 1970s. My *Debunking Economics* (Keen 2011) collates a century's worth of criticism that Neoclassical economics has ignored, and whose consequences it has evaded via ludicrous assumptions, only a handful of which I outlined in the previous chapter. Organizations like the Institute for New Economic Thinking provide online courses in alternative economic thought, and student movements like Rethinking Economics mean that, as a rebel, 'you'll never walk alone' – you'll know you're not the only one dissatisfied with the conventional curriculum at your university, and eager to learn of alternatives.

The most important alternative approaches to economics that you should learn are Post Keynesian economics, Modern Monetary Theory, and Biophysical Economics. The development of the Post Keynesian school of thought was driven by an abhorrence of the unrealism underpinning Neoclassical economics, and it has provided many powerful insights that can form the basis of realistic, non-equilibrium, system dynamics models of the economy and ecology. Foremost here, in my mind, are the models of Richard Goodwin (Goodwin 1966, 1967, 1982, 1986a, 1986b; Goodwin and Punzo 1987; Goodwin et al. 1986), and Wynne Godley (Godley 1999, 2004; Godley and Lavoie 2007; Lavoie and Godley 2001), and the verbal models of Hyman Minsky (Minsky 1963, 1972, 1977, 1982) that formed the basis of my own modelling (Barnett et al. 2000; Keen 1995, 2000, 2013b, 2015b, 2020b).

There is also a wealth of other insights from Post Keynesian economics that should inform your modelling, including Kalecki's original engineering-based models (Kalecki 1935, 1937, 1941, 1949, 1962, 1968, 1971), and Sraffa's meticulous multi-sectoral modelling, whose dynamic promise has still not been properly explored (Keen 1998; Sraffa 1960, 1962; Steedman 1992, 1993).

There are excellent books documenting Post Keynesian economics, of which the outstanding ones are Marc Lavoie's *Post-Keynesian Economics: New Foundations* (Lavoie 2015a) for a macroeconomic perspective and Fred Lee's *Microeconomic Theory: A Heterodox Approach* (Lee 2018) for a micro perspective. There are journals dedicated to the Post Keynesian approach, most notably the *Journal of Post Keynesian Economics*, the *Review of Political Economy*, and the *Review of Keynesian Economics*. John King provides a scholarly overview of the history of Post Keynesian economics (King 2003, 2012, 2014). I also strongly recommend the mathematician John Blatt's recently re-published masterpiece *Dynamic Economic Systems: A Post Keynesian Approach* (Blatt 1983).

There is one significant caveat as regards existing Post Keynesian economic models: the overwhelming majority of these are expressed in 'discrete time' form. This partly reflects the Neoclassical education most Post Keynesian economists acquired in their youth: almost all Neoclassical models use 'difference equations' – where variables are given values at times t, $t + 1$, $t + 2$, etc. (Sargent and Stachurski 2020a, 2020b)[2] – rather than differential equations, where models are in terms of the rates of change of variables with respect to time. Post Keynesian economists sometimes argue that this method is necessitated by the nature of economic data, which comes in discrete time steps (as yearly or quarterly data estimates). But Forrester, who was arguably *the* authority on dynamic modelling, was emphatic that this is completely wrong:

> The incremental time intervals for which the variables of a model are solved step-by-step in time must be much shorter than often supposed … This solution interval is unrelated to the interval at which national statistics and economic indicators are measured. (Forrester 2003, pp. 337–45)

Discrete time is only really appropriate at the macro level for processes that are highly synchronous – such as the synchronized birth of some animal species, where the synchronization is an evolutionary survival mechanism. In economics, while each individual transaction is discrete, each is also asynchronous with respect to other transactions: all investments don't occur at the same time, but a difference equation setup assumes that they do. In a 'top down' model, aggregate asynchronous phenomena are far more realistically modelled using continuous time than discrete time.

The time delays in discrete time economic models are also normally quite arbitrary. They are almost always in terms of years, which is a reasonable timeframe for investment, but not for consumption, where the scale should be in terms of weeks or months rather than years. To do discrete time modelling properly, consumption in period t should be modelled as depending on income in period $t - 2$ (say), where the time period is measured in weeks, while investment in period t should be modelled as depending on the change in income between period $t - 26$ and $t - 52$ (say).

However, no-one actually does this, because it is simply too complicated: in practice, lags of one year are the rule in macroeconomic discrete time models. Secondly, if a discrete time model were done properly, and empirical work later found that investment in period t actually depended on the change in income between period $t - 40$ and $t - 86$ (say), then the entire structure of the model would need to be re-written. This is not necessary for a continuous time model, where the equivalent function to a time delay is a time lag, which is represented by a simple scalar that can be altered easily.

Modern Monetary Theory is the other major area of modern non-Neoclassical economics that you need to master, and there are now excellent resources on this, including most importantly Kelton's very accessible *The Deficit Myth* (Kelton 2020), the MMT textbook *Macroeconomics* by Mitchell, Wray and Watts (Mitchell et al. 2019), and the blog New Economic Perspectives. There are also many other important initiatives in non-Neoclassical economics today, including the work of Ole Peters and colleagues in developing non-ergodic economic and financial analysis (Peters 2019), with precursor work by J. Edgar Peters (Peters 1994, 1996, 2003) and Mandelbrot (Mandelbrot and Hudson 2004). You can explore ecological economics at the website of The International Society for Ecological Economics.

Biophysical economics (Bobulescu 2015; Daly 1991b; Fontana and Sawyer 2016; Hall 2011; Hall et al. 2001) does not have as cohesive a canon as Post Keynesian

Economics or MMT, but this may change rapidly in the near future. In the meantime, you should read the work on energy and economics by numerous authors, including those above and Ayres et al. (2013), Boulding (1992, 2009), Cleveland et al. (2001), Costanza et al. (1997), Daly (1997, 1999, 2007), Daly and Farley (2011), Garrett (2014), Georgescu-Roegen (1999, 2004), Keen et al. (2019), Kümmel (2011) and Voudouris et al. (2015).

There are many online resources on heterodox economics in general, with sites like the Heterodox Economics Newsletter and INET's History of Economic Thought website. You can also keep in touch with my own contributions at my Patreon page www.patreon.com/profstevekeen, where all but the podcasts are freely accessible.

Also consider doing a degree that lets you tailor your education, rather than one like a standard Economics degree with its unavoidable Neoclassical core,[3] and compulsory ancillary units in Econometrics and the like. I did a combined Arts/Law degree where the Arts component let me choose any Humanities, Science or Economics subjects, so I majored in Economics while also doing Mathematics and Psychology. The Mathematics in particular was invaluable, and it was one of the major reasons I became a heterodox economist: I could see how flimsy the mathematical foundations of Neoclassical economics were – and conventional labour-theory-of-value Marxism, for that matter (Keen 1993a, 1993b).

If you do a degree in Economics, do so in a way that allows you to take as many courses from outside the economics faculty as possible. Use your electives to study mathematics, computing, thermodynamics, ecology and history from the experts, rather than doing more courses taught by Neoclassical economists. You could also major in mathematics, computing, engineering or system dynamics directly, and then independently teach yourself the fraction of economics that is actually worth learning, via online resources and critical books.

There is much more to a completely new paradigm for economics than I could cover in this book. But I hope there is enough here for you to see a way in which you can help bring it about, while there is still a chance that the economic system itself can survive the ecological crisis that Neoclassical economics has, in large measure, doomed us to in the coming decades.

I close this book by looking back on one of the most important books in my own intellectual development, John Blatt's *Dynamic Economic Systems: A Post-Keynesian Approach* (Blatt 1983).[4] Blatt was not, in fact, an economist, but a mathematician who, after a distinguished career in mathematics and physics, was accidentally exposed to advanced Neoclassical economics. He was horrified by what he saw, and especially, by its obsession with equilibrium modelling. Speaking with the authority of a leading figure in mathematical dynamics, he observed in the Introduction to *Dynamic Economic Systems* that:

> At present, the state of our dynamic economics is more akin to a crawl than to a walk, to say nothing of a run. *Indeed, some may think that capitalism as a social system may disappear before its dynamics are understood by economists.* (Blatt 1983, pp. 4–5, emphasis added)

When I first read this in 1991, I thought it was a good piece of hyperbole. I now regard it as a depressingly prescient prediction. Given the role that Neoclassical economists have played in humanity making only trivial responses to the challenge of climate change to date, the social system that gets us through that challenge – if we do get through it – will be far more a command than a market economy. For this reason, I regard Neoclassical economics as not merely a bad methodology for economic analysis, but as an existential threat to the continued existence of capitalism – and human civilization in general. It has to go.

Notes

Chapter 1

1 It is often also called 'mainstream economics'. There are divisions within Neoclassical economics, especially between self-described 'New Classicals' and 'New Keynesians'. Even more confusingly, some 'New Keynesians' claim that they are not 'Neoclassical', and in fact use it as a term of abuse towards 'New Classicals'.

2 The campaign was supported by 300 of the registered 1,800 academic economists in France, one-third of whom were economic historians, while the rest were economists.

3 The one exception was Robert Shiller, recipient of the Economics Nobel Prize in 2013. But Shiller's prediction relied not upon a Neoclassical economic model, but on his excellent historical and statistical research, which diverges substantially from mainstream Neoclassical thinking.

4 Axel Leijonhufvud's 'Life among the Econ' is a brilliant satire of the discipline of economics. If you haven't yet read it, put this book down now and do so. As well as giving you a good laugh, it will prepare you for the pompous dismissal that this book will receive from Neoclassical economists.

5 This is not to suggest that physics always achieves the resolution implied here, nor that the process is fast or straightforward, as Peter Woit details in his critique of string

theory in the book *Not Even Wrong* (Woit 2006), and on his blog.

6 I'm also partial to the arguments of Feyerabend and Lakatos on this topic, but Kuhn's masterful analysis of the scientific method is the reference to read if you are interested in how science progresses.

7 IS-LM stands for 'Investment-Savings-Liquidity-Money'.

8 Hicks abandoned his Neoclassical beliefs in later life, and explained that his misinterpretation of Keynes arose from his Neoclassical model (developed in Hicks 1935) having a time period of a week – a period over which expectations could be assumed to be constant. Keynes, however, worked in terms of years, a period over which expectations were bound to change. This invalidated Hicks's LM curve, because 'there is no sense in liquidity, unless expectations are uncertain' (Hicks 1981, p. 152). He also strongly rejected the use of equilibrium modelling techniques.

9 The obsession with equilibrium as a mathematical state of the economy has led to exalting it as desirable as well. Certainly, as I explain in the next chapter, the financial instability of capitalism is a serious weakness. But as Schumpeter argued almost a century ago (Schumpeter 1928), instability is one of the strengths of industrial capitalism, not a weakness: it leads to the innovation and change that is the essential strength of capitalism, compared to other social systems. The fact that the system is out of equilibrium all the time is partly because of, and partly the motivation for, entrepreneurial activity.

10 There were and still are Austrian and Marxist Schools of Economics, but the former shares many of the same foundations as Neoclassical economics – dropping primarily the emphasis upon equilibrium – while the latter has fundamental problems of its own that it has never properly resolved (see Keen 1993a, 1993b).

11 The other key student leaders of this revolt were Richard Fields and Richard Osborne in 1973, and Mike Brezniak and Rod O'Donnell in 1974–76. Only Rod and I continued on to academic careers.

12 In a curious historical parallel, the appointment of the University of Manchester Professor of Economics Bruce Williams as Vice-Chancellor of Sydney University in the late

1960s was pivotal to the outbreak of the dispute at Sydney University.

Chapter 2

1 In a delicious irony, Bernanke found himself in charge of the Federal Reserve when 'It' – a crisis akin to the Great Depression – happened again in 2007.

2 The Bank of England papers cited the Post Keynesian authors Nicholas Kaldor, Basil Moore, Thomas Palley, Josh Ryan-Collins, Richard Werner and Andrew Jackson, as well as Michael Kumhof, who is arguably the only Neoclassical economist to both understand that banks create money, and to appreciate its macroeconomic significance.

3 This includes the 10th edition, published in 2019.

4 The exception to this rule is Michael Kumhof of the Bank of England.

5 As the anthropologist David Graeber pointed out, the vision promulgated by economists from the time of Adam Smith on, of ancient economies that used barter evolving into money-using economies today, is a myth: 'The story, then, is everywhere. It is the founding myth of our system of economic relations. It is so deeply established in common sense, even in places like Madagascar, that most people on earth couldn't imagine any other way that money possibly could have come about. The problem is there's no evidence that it ever happened, and an enormous amount of evidence suggesting that it did not. For centuries now, explorers have been trying to find this fabled land of barter – none with success' (Graeber 2011).

6 Godley Tables can have multiple equity accounts, to enable modelling of short-term and long-term equity, but in this book, for simplicity, I only consider a single short-term equity account.

7 There are some assets – such as consumer durables that you own outright – which are an asset to you and a liability to no-one else. In this book, I model only financial claims that are assets to one person and liabilities to another, so that the sum of all equity is necessarily zero.

8 Irony alert.

9 In this simple model, where no distinction is made between short-term (at-call) and long-term bank equity, the money supply includes bank equity. A more sophisticated model would have payments made to an at-call account of the banking sector.

10 I did not fully appreciate this point myself, prior to reading Stephanie Kelton's *The Deficit Myth* (Kelton 2020), and then building *Minsky* models to check – and confirm – her argument. Before then, if asked whether deficits created money, I would sometimes answer 'to the extent that they are monetized by the central bank'. As you will soon see, central bank bond purchases are irrelevant to money creation.

11 The construct of the 'banking sector' lumps together many independent financial institutions. In the real world the part of the banking sector that actually buys Treasury Bonds are called 'primary dealers'. Some are banks, whose reserves are directly increased when the government net spends on its account holders; others are merchant banks and the like who might need to borrow reserves from banks.

12 See https://en.wikipedia.org/wiki/Debt_monetization: 'Debt monetization or monetary finance is the practice of a government borrowing money from the central bank, which, in the process of buying the debt, creates new money. It is one of the practices often informally called printing money. This practice allows a government to finance its deficit without creating money directly – which is prohibited in many countries – and also without increasing debt to private parties.'

13 As with selling bonds to the central bank, the banks only make such sales if they profit from them, and these trading profits aren't shown here, though they could easily be included in a more elaborate model.

14 Whether it generates real wealth depends, in our modern fiat world, on how much it causes under-utilized capacity to be used, versus how much it could drive up prices or generate a trade deficit. For those who know MMT well, this last comment indicates that I reject the MMT position on foreign trade, which I interpret as encouraging trade deficits. This aspect of MMT is not derived from its monetary insights, but from the aphorism that 'Imports are real benefits and

exports are real costs' (Mosler 2010, p. 59), which I believe contradicts MMT's monetary insights.

15 Phillips' work has been badly misinterpreted – even on the usual standards of Neoclassical scholarship. He was in fact one of the pioneers of dynamic modelling in economics, and his work was on a par with, and possibly even more advanced than, Forrester's at the same time. See Phillips (1950, 1954, 1956, 1957, 1959, 1968) for his work on building dynamic economic models using techniques adapted from engineering.

16 The argument that the Federal Reserve alone controls the rate of money growth is the reason that Friedman ignored two obvious triggers to high inflation during the 1970s, the two OPEC-inspired hikes in the price of oil, firstly in 1973 (marked on figures 2.7 and 2.8) after the Yom Kippur War, and then again in 1979 after the Iranian Revolution (at the same time as Volcker formally implemented monetarism, also marked on figures 2.7 and 2.8). Both events quadrupled its price, from $2.50 a barrel to $10 in 1973, and from $10 to $40 in 1979. Monetarist dogma ignored this by insisting that causation runs solely from the money supply to prices; reality instead shows that causation works both ways, with – as Moore explains in 'The Endogenous Money Stock' (Moore 1979) – changes in wages and raw material prices leading to growth in the money supply.

17 Total monetary income is higher than shown in a Moore Table, because it excludes spending internal to a sector – manufacturers spending on other manufacturers, etc. However, in the limit – when all entities in an economy are treated separately – then a Moore Table captures total aggregate income and expenditure.

18 The amounts A, B, etc. in table 2.3 don't have to be the same numerical amounts as in table 2.2.

19 Though their orbits, like that of all astronomical bodies, are also chaotic, as Poincare proved in 1899.

20 Figure 2.9 combines data from the Bank of International Settlements from 1952 with data from the US Census from 1916 till 1970 (Census Bureau 1975, tables X398 and X580). The data series are different in composition and scale, but they fortunately overlap (BIS/Federal Reserve data cover 1946 till today; one Census series covers 1916

till 1970; the other covers 1834 till 1970), and the rates of change are very similar. The data in figure 2.9 rescale the two earlier series to match the scale of the BIS data.

21 After the 1929 stock market crash, the maximum level of gearing was reduced to 50 per cent – so that $1,000 could purchase a portfolio valued at $2,000.

22 Using Robert Shiller's conservative share market valuation series, the Cyclically Adjusted Price to Earnings ratio: see http://www.econ.yale.edu/~shiller/data.htm.

23 I should note that Richard is both a friend, and one of the most generous of my approximately 1,500 supporters on Patreon at https://www.patreon.com/ProfSteveKeen.

24 These loans need not cede any management control to banks, something many entrepreneurs have told me they dread, given the short-term focus of bankers and their lack of technical knowledge outside finance itself.

Chapter 3

1 It actually has two, with the equilibrium of zero predators and zero prey being unstable.

2 Mainstream economics has been constructed as if only the first two possibilities exist, which is why they persist with the false assumption that a system's equilibrium – the point you converge to in the first case – is stable.

3 In the next chapter I show that it is the energy that capital turns into useful work that determines output. As I show in *Modelling with Minsky*, this is consistent with the models in this chapter, because what is called the 'capital to output ratio' in these models is actually the efficiency with which energy is turned into useful work.

4 Other factors, such as a target level of capacity utilization, could have been used in the investment equation, but would have resulted in a more complicated model, when the intention was to build the simplest possible model. The uncertainty of the future, in Keynes's sense, turns up here in the overly strong reliance both workers and capitalists make upon current conditions, as expressed in the current level of employment and the current level of profits: 'It would be foolish, in forming our expectations, to attach great

weight to matters which are very uncertain. It is reasonable, therefore, to be guided to a considerable degree by the facts about which we feel somewhat confident, even though they may be less decisively relevant to the issue than other facts about which our knowledge is vague and scanty. For this reason the facts of the existing situation enter, in a sense disproportionately, into the formation of our long-term expectations; our usual practice being to take the existing situation and to project it into the future, modified only to the extent that we have more or less definite reasons for expecting a change' (Keynes 1936, Chapter 12).

5 Most complex systems can be approximated by a polynomial, which is derived from the original model using what is known as a Taylor series expansion. The linear part of this is the coefficient for the term in x. The nonlinear part are the terms in x squared, x cubed, and so on.

6 Consequently, the stability of a model with an unstable equilibrium can't be 'saved' by adding more complicated terms to it: it's the simplest terms that make it unstable.

7 There is a typesetting error in one of the equations in the 1995 paper that turned a negative into a positive. If you wish to explore this model yourself, please use the equations in the 2020 paper instead.

8 The recorded rate of unemployment drastically understates the actual level, and all changes to the formal definition have reduced the recorded level: not one has caused the recorded level to rise.

9 The lower recorded peak level of unemployment in 2010 than 1983 was due to redefinitions of unemployment since 1983. If the pre-1983 definition had been used in 2010, the recorded unemployment rate would have been substantially higher.

10 It is easy enough to find on the Web, for example at https://www.asc.ohio-state.edu/jayaprakash.1/880/moreisdifferent.pdf.

11 Give an extra $1,000 to SpaceX owner Elon Musk, and on his word, he will spend at least $500 of it on establishing a future human outpost on Mars – see https://twitter.com/elonmusk/status/1050812486226599936?s=20. A thousand dollars going to a homeless person would be spent on things for the here and now.

12 Technically, it can have any shape you can fit with a continuous function, like a polynomial – an equation of the form $y = a + bx + cx^2 + \dots + zx^n$. That's any curve you can draw with a pen where you (a) don't take the pen off the page, (b) don't cross the curve at any point and (c) don't draw above it so that there are two or more y values for one x value. This is not to say that demand curves one might construct from economic data would have 'any shape at all', but rather that Neoclassical economists cannot explain one fundamental aspect of their theory, the 'Law of Demand'.

13 For example, the assumption that the relationship between capital and output is a constant. The ratio is actually declining, but slowly: it has been between 3.9 and 3.1 for the United States for the last seventy years – see https://myf. red/g/vRx1. I'll address how to interpret this relationship in the next chapter. Investment could be made to depend on other factors as well – such as a target level of capacity utilization, which is a common assumption in Post Keynesian models.

14 There are also serious problems about defining an aggregate amount of capital, which the references given here explore in what was known as 'the Cambridge Controversies'. They are more damaging to Neoclassical economics than other approaches because Neoclassical theory asserts that the quantity of capital determines the return to capital. That problem of a circular definition does not apply to the models in this chapter, where the return to capital is a residual after wages and interest payments have been deducted.

Chapter 4

1 The Cobb–Douglas production function is $Y = A \times K^\alpha \times L^{1-\alpha}$, where Y represents real output per year (in fictional units of a standard commodity, often called 'widgets'), A represents the state of technology at a point in time (and is called 'total factor productivity' in the Neoclassical literature), K is the 'number' of machines and L the number of workers, and α is a number between 0 and 1 that represents the contribution of capital to production (generally is set at 0.25–0.3). The Leontief production function is $Y = u \times \dfrac{K}{v} = a \times L$, where u is

a number between 0 and 1 representing the fraction of the capital stock in use, v is the 'capital to output ratio', which is a measured parameter lying between 2 and 4 for most countries – and a is the output to labour ratio. Both can be combined using what is called a CES ('constant elasticity of substitution') function, but in general Neoclassicals use the Cobb–Douglas form and Post Keynesians use the Leontief.

2 The logic behind these laws is difficult, even for experts, but they were well summarized in a joke by the poet Alan Ginsberg: '1. You can't win; 2. You can't break even; 3. You can't even get out of the game'. Ginsberg's first point captures the First Law of Thermodynamics, which is that energy can neither be created nor destroyed: we can't 'make' energy, we can only use what exists. The second expresses the Second Law, which is the hardest to characterize without mathematics: for economic analysis, we can paraphrase it as 'using energy to do work generates waste'. Ginsberg's third quip encapsulates the Third Law, that the only way to avoid waste energy from work is to find a location where the temperature is absolute zero (–273.15°C, or –459.67°F) – and there is no such place.

3 The causation clearly goes both ways – the quadrupling of oil prices in 1973 and again in 1979 played a large role in the recessions during those years, while the GFC caused a large drop in energy consumption in 2006–10.

4 *Modelling with Minsky*, the free online companion to this book, includes preliminary models based on production using energy, and production using energy and matter, using this insight.

5 The functional form of both models is revised from $Y(t)=F(L(t),K(t))$ to $Q(t)=F(L(E(t)),K(E(t)))$, where $Q(t)$ represents output in terms of useful work, while $L(E(t))$ and $K(E(t))$ represent the energy harnessed by labour and capital, respectively, to perform useful work. Both are expanded to represent the number of machines (K) and workers (L), multiplied by the energy consumption per unit per year (E_L and E_K), times how efficiently this energy is turned into useful work (e_L and e_K). Thus $L(E(t))=L{\times}E_L{\times}e_L$ and $K(E(t))=K{\times}E_K{\times}e_K$. The product $E_L{\times}e_L$ is treated as a constant C_L, since while the energy consumption per person has risen radically since industrialization began in

the late 1700s, the energy output that a typical worker can sustain in employment has not changed – while the energy consumption and output of a typical machine has risen radically. With these alterations, the Cobb–Douglas function becomes $Q=C_L \cdot (E_K \cdot e_K)^\alpha \cdot K^\alpha \cdot L^{1-\alpha}$, and the Leontief function becomes $Q=u \cdot K \cdot E_K \cdot e_K$. The Cobb–Douglas form shows that what Neoclassical economists call 'total factor productivity' is actually the energy consumption of the 'representative machine' at a given time. The Leontief form implies that the 'capital to output ratio' (v) in the standard Leontief function is actually the inverse of e_K. In this sense, the Leontief function has implicitly incorporated the role of energy in production.

6 The atmospheric physicist Tim Garrett has derived a model of human civilization as a heat engine, exploiting the high potential energy of fossil fuel reserves to enable civilization to exist at a higher level of potential energy than the ecology in which it is embedded. From this he derives a relationship between GDP and change in energy usage, where his empirical fit is even stronger than the one that I show in figure 4.2 between change in energy and change in GDP. We are working together to see if we can make our two approaches compatible.

7 If you dispute that this is inevitable, with thoughts of the 'digital economy' or 'decoupling', take another look at figure 4.2, which shows the correlation of change in energy with change in GDP for the last half century. It is 0.83. There would have to be a huge change in the energy to GDP relationship for decoupling to happen, and I'm going to call that assumption a fantasy, rather than a scientific conjecture.

8 This is even without considering the addition of greenhouse gases to the atmosphere, which is the basis of global warming.

9 The less than 1.5°C increase we have already caused may well be the ultimate cause of the volatile weather that struck the United States in February 2021, when all of Texas experienced temperatures below 0°C: see https://www.nytimes.com/interactive/2021/02/16/us/winter-storm-map.html.

10 When one controls for other factors apart from latitude, such as altitude, rainfall, distance from the ocean, etc.

11 K stands for 'Kelvin', which is the temperature scale measured from absolute zero, and 1K is equal to 1°C.

12 See https://data.giss.nasa.gov/gistemp/maps/, where you can calculate temperature anomaly estimates for different time periods, and their distribution by latitude from the South to the North Pole.

Chapter 5

1 The most telling example here is Alan Blinder's book *Asking about Prices*. Blinder is a key member of the economic mainstream, and yet his book has been utterly ignored. In contrast to over a hundred reviews on Amazon for Mas-Colell's *Microeconomics* textbook, there is just one review of Blinder's empirically grounded book – *and I wrote it*. Neoclassical economists blissfully ignore inconvenient truths. Ironically, this even includes Blinder, who does not cite his own research in his microeconomics textbook.

2 My favourite instance of such an assumption occurs in the hallowed *Theory of Value*, by Nobel Prize recipient Gerard Debreu. For decades the Arrow–Debreu framework was the 'gold standard' of economic reasoning. Here is how Debreu handles the future: 'For a producer ... a production plan (*made now for the whole future*) is a specification of the quantities of all his inputs and all his outputs ... *The certainty assumption implies that he knows now what input-output combinations will be possible in the future (although he may not know now the details of the technical processes which will make them possible)*' (Debreu 1959, pp. 37–8). His extension to an uncertain future results in 'a theory of uncertainty free from any probability concept and formally identical with the theory of certainty developed in the preceding chapters' (Debreu 1959, p. 98).

3 My paper 'A Monetary Minsky Model of the Great Moderation and the Great Recession' was rejected, without refereeing, by the editor of the *American Economic Review: Macro*, because I did not assume rational expectations. In a heated email exchange after that rejection, the editor at one point stated, without irony, 'but what if they get

more information about the future? How will that change things?'. Information, about the future. Yeah, right...

Chapter 6

1 If you want to bring about a new paradigm in economics, then I urge you to use *Minsky*, and join our beta testers program to help improve it over time. You can also sign up to its Patreon page https://www.patreon.com/hpcoder/, or support it indirectly via my Patreon page https://www.patreon.com/ProfSteveKeen. The models in this book, and *Minsky*'s user interface, are documented in the free companion to this book, *Modelling with Minsky*.

2 Sargent's two *Macroeconomics with Python* textbooks have only a handful of differential equation models in their nearly 2,000 pages.

3 Speaking of cores, the so-called CORE textbook is a public-relations-oriented repackaging of standard Neoclassical economics. For example, its section on individual behaviour is straight indifference curve/revealed preference thinking; its defense of this model cites Milton Friedman's dodgy 'as if' methodology; and it makes no reference to a conclusive experiment that shows this theory does not work as a model of human behaviour – 'as if' or otherwise (Sippel 1997).

4 Blatt's exposition of Goodwin's growth cycle model was much clearer than Goodwin's original, and this model became the basis of my model of Minsky's Financial Instability Hypothesis. Blatt's explanations of the mathematical instability of general equilibrium and the fallacies in expected utility theory are also first class.

References

Anderson PW (1972) More Is Different. *Science* 177 (4047): 393–6

Andresen T (2018) On the Dynamics of Money Circulation, Creation and Debt – A Control Systems Approach. Norwegian University of Science and Technology, Trondheim

Arent DJ, Tol RSJ, Faust E, Hella JP, Kumar S, Strzepek KM, Tóth FL, Yan D (2014) Key Economic Sectors and Services. In: Field CB, Barros VR, Dokken DJ, et al. (eds) *Climate Change 2014: Impacts, Adaptation, and Vulnerability. Part A: Global and Sectoral Aspects. Contribution of Working Group II to the Fifth Assessment Report of the Intergovernmental Panel on Climate Change.* Cambridge: Cambridge University Press, pp 659–708

Aristotle (350 BCE [1952]) *Meteorologica* (trans HDP Lee). London: Heinemann

Arrow KJ, Intriligator MD, Hildenbrand W, Sonnenschein H (1981–1993) *Handbook of Mathematical Economics.* Amsterdam: North-Holland

Ayres RU (1978) Application of Physical Principles to Economics. In: Ayers RU (ed) *Resources, Environment, and Economics: Applications of the Materials/Energy Balance Principle.* Chichester: John Wiley & Sons, Chapter 3

Ayres RU, Voudouris V (2014) The Economic Growth Enigma: Capital, Labour and Useful Energy? *Energy Policy* 64: 16–28. http://dx.doi.org/10.1016/j.enpol.2013.06.001

Ayres RU, van den Bergh JCJM, Lindenberger D, Warr B (2013) The Underestimated Contribution of Energy to Economic Growth. *Structural Change and Economic Dynamics* 27: 79–88. https://doi.org/10.1016/j.strueco.2013.07.004

Backhouse RE (1988) The Value of Post Keynesian Economics: A Neoclassical Response to Harcourt and Hamouda. *Bulletin of Economic Research* 40 (1): 35–41. https://doi.org/10.1111/j.1467-8586.1988.tb00252.x

Bardi U (2018) Why Economists Can't Understand Complex Systems: Not Even the Nobel Prize, William Nordhaus. https://cassandralegacy.blogspot.com/2018/10/why-economists-cant-understand-complex.html

Barnett WA, Chiarella C, Keen S, Marks R, Schnabl H (2000) *Commerce, Complexity, and Evolution: Topics in Economics, Finance, Marketing, and Management: Proceedings of the Twelfth International Symposium in Economic Theory and Econometrics.* New York: Cambridge University Press

Bell S (2000) Do Taxes and Bonds Finance Government Spending? *Journal of Economic Issues* 34 (3): 603–20. https://doi.org/10.1080/00213624.2000.11506296

Bell S (2001) The Role of the State and the Hierarchy of Money. *Cambridge Journal of Economics* 25 (2): 149–63. https://doi.org/10.1093/cje/25.2.149

Bernanke BS (2000) *Essays on the Great Depression.* Princeton, NJ: Princeton University Press

Bernanke BS (2004a) The Great Moderation: Remarks by Governor Ben S. Bernanke At the meetings of the Eastern Economic Association, Washington, DC,

February 20, 2004. Paper presented at the Eastern Economic Association, Washington, DC

Bernanke BS (2004b) Panel discussion: What Have We Learned Since October 1979? In: *Conference on Reflections on Monetary Policy 25 Years after October 1979*. St. Louis, MO: Federal Reserve Bank of St. Louis

Bernanke BS (2010) Aiding the Economy: What the Fed Did and Why. *The Washington Post*, 5 November

Bezemer DJ (2009a) 'No One Saw This Coming' – Or Did They? Centre for Economic Policy Research (CEPR). https://voxeu.org/article/no-one-saw-coming-or-did-they

Bezemer DJ (2009b) 'No One Saw This Coming': Understanding Financial Crisis Through Accounting Models. Faculty of Economics, University of Groningen, Groningen, The Netherlands

Bezemer DJ (2010) Understanding Financial Crisis Through Accounting Models. *Accounting, Organizations and Society* 35 (7): 676–88. https://doi.org/10.1016/j.aos.2010.07.002

Bezemer DJ, Grydaki M (2014) Financial Fragility in the Great Moderation. *Journal of Banking & Finance* 49: 169–77. https://doi.org/10.1016/j.jbankfin.2014.09.005

Blanchard O (2016) Do DSGE Models Have a Future? Peterson Institute for International Economics

Blanchard O (2018) On the Future of Macroeconomic Models. *Oxford Review of Economic Policy* 34 (1–2): 43–54. https://doi.org/10.1093/oxrep/grx045

Blatt JM (1983) *Dynamic Economic Systems: A Post-Keynesian Approach*. New York: Routledge

Blinder AS (1998) *Asking about Prices: A New Approach to Understanding Price Stickiness*. New York: Russell Sage Foundation

Bobulescu R (2015) From Lotka's Biophysics to Georgescu-Roegen's Bioeconomics. *Ecological Economics* 120: 194–202. http://dx.doi.org/10.1016/j.ecolecon.2015.10.016

Bossel H (1994) *Modeling and Simulation.* Boca Raton, FL: Taylor & Francis

Boulding KE (1973) The Economics of Energy. *Annals of the American Academy of Political and Social Science* 410: 120–6. https://doi.org/10.1177/000271627341000112

Boulding KE (1992) The Economics of the Coming Spaceship Earth. In: Markandya A, Richardson J (eds) *Environmental Economics: A Reader.* New York: St. Martin's Press, pp 27–35

Boulding KE (2009) The Economics of the Coming Spaceship Earth. In: Brooks RRW, Keohane NO, Kysar DA (eds) *Economics of Environmental Law. Volume 1. Theoretical Foundations.* Cheltenham: Elgar, pp 433–44

Braun M (1993) *Differential Equations and Their Applications: An Introduction to Applied Mathematics.* New York: Springer

Burke M, Hsiang SM, Miguel E (2015) Global Non-Linear Effect of Temperature on Economic Production. *Nature* 527 (7577): 235. https://doi.org/10.1038/nature15725

Butler G, Jones E, Stilwell F (2009) *Political Economy Now!: The Struggle for Alternative Economics at the University of Sydney.* Sydney: Darlington Press

Cantillon R (1755) *An Essay on Economic Theory* (trans C Saucier; ed M Thornton). Auburn, AL: Ludwig von Mises Institute

Census Bureau (1949) *Historical Statistics of the United States 1789–1945.* Washington, DC: United States Government

Census Bureau (1975) *Historical Statistics of the United States Colonial Times to 1970.* Washington, DC: United States Government

Cleveland CJ, Stern DI, Costanza R (2001) *The Economics of Nature and the Nature of Economics.* Cheltenham: Elgar

Coase RH (1988) *The Firm, the Market and the Law.* Chicago, IL: University of Chicago Press

Cobb CW, Douglas PH (1928) A Theory of Production.

The American Economic Review 18 (1): 139–65. https://doi.org/10.2307/1811556

Coolidge C (1928) 1928 State of the Union Address, 4 December. https://coolidgefoundation.org/resources/sixth-annual-message-to-the-congress-of-the-united-states/

Coppola F (2019) *People's Quantitative Easing.* Cambridge: Polity

Cornell CE, Black RA, Xue M, Litz HE, Ramsay A, Gordon M, Mileant A, Cohen ZR, Williams JA, Lee KK, Drobny GP, Keller SL (2019) Prebiotic Amino Acids Bind to and Stabilize Prebiotic Fatty Acid Membranes. *Proceedings of the National Academy of Sciences* 116 (35): 17239–44. https://doi.org/10.1073/pnas.1900275116

Costa Lima B, Grasselli MR, Wang XS, Wu J (2014) Destabilizing a Stable Crisis: Employment Persistence and Government Intervention in Macroeconomics. *Structural Change and Economic Dynamics* 30 (1): 30–51. http://dx.doi.org/10.1016/j.strueco.2014.02.003

Costanza R, Perrings C, Cleveland CJ (1997) *The Development of Ecological Economics.* Cheltenham: Elgar

Cotis J-P (2007) Editorial: Achieving Further Rebalancing. In: OECD (ed) *OECD Economic Outlook*, vol 2007/1. Paris: OECD, pp 7–10. doi:10.1787/eco_outlook-v2007-1-2-en

Daly HE (1991a) The Concept of a Steady-State Economy. In: Daly HE (ed) *Steady-State Economics*. Washington, DC: Island Press, pp 14–49

Daly HE (1991b) Conclusion: On Biophysical Equilibrium and Moral Growth. In: Daly HE (ed) *Steady-State Economics*. Washington, DC: Island Press, pp 168–78

Daly HE (1997) Sustainable Growth: An Impossibility Theorem. *Development* 40 (1): 121–5

Daly HE (1999) On Economics as a Life Science. In: Ayres RU, Button K, Nijkamp P (eds) *Global Aspects of the Environment*, 2 vols. Cheltenham: Elgar, pp 45–59

Daly HE (2007) Ecological Economic Theory: An Overview. In: Erickson JD, Gowdy JM (eds) *Frontiers in Ecological Economic Theory and Application.* Cheltenham: Elgar, pp 3–6

Daly HE (2009) Sustainability Is an Objective Value. In: Boersema JJ, Reijnders L (eds) *Principles of Environmental Sciences.* New York: Springer, pp 483–90

Daly HE, Farley J (2011) *Ecological Economics: Principles and Applications.* Washington, DC: Island Press

De Vroey M (1975) The Transition from Classical to Neoclassical Economics: A Scientific Revolution. *Journal of Economic Issues* 9 (3): 415–39. http://dx.doi.org/10.1080/00213624.1975.11503296

Debreu G (1959) *Theory of Value: An Axiomatic Analysis of Economic Equilibrium.* New Haven, CT: Yale University Press

DeCanio SJ (2003) *Economic Models of Climate Change: A Critique.* New York: Palgrave Macmillan

Desan C (2015) *Making Money: Coin, Currency, and the Coming of Capitalism.* Oxford: Oxford University Press

Deutsche Bundesbank (2017) The Role of Banks, Non-Banks and the Central Bank in the Money Creation Process. Deutsche Bundesbank Monthly Report, April: 13–33

Downward P (1994) A Reappraisal of Case Study Evidence on Business Pricing: A Comparison of Neoclassical and Post Keynesian Perspectives. *British Review of Economic Issues* 16 (39): 23–43

Eddington AS (1928) *The Nature of the Physical World.* Cambridge: Cambridge University Press

Einstein A (1934) On the Method of Theoretical Physics. *Philosophy of Science* 1 (2): 163–9

Eiteman WJ (1947) Factors Determining the Location of the Least Cost Point. *The American Economic Review* 37 (5): 910–18

Eiteman WJ, Guthrie GE (1952) The Shape of the Average

Cost Curve. *The American Economic Review* 42 (5): 832–8

Elliott L (2017) Heretics Welcome! Economics Needs a New Reformation. *The Guardian*, 17 December

Feher DC (2019) A Synthesis of Behavioural Economics and Minsky's Financial Instability Hypothesis: An Agent-Based Simulation Exploration of Satisficing Behaviours in a Complex Financial Economy. PhD thesis, University of Sydney, Sydney

Fisher I (1929) Fisher Sees Stocks Permanently High. *New York Times*, 16 October

Fisher I (1932) *Booms and Depressions: Some First Principles.* New York: Adelphi

Fisher I (1933) The Debt-Deflation Theory of Great Depressions. *Econometrica* 1 (4): 337–57

Fontana G, Realfonzo R (eds) (2005) *The Monetary Theory of Production: Tradition and Perspectives.* Basingstoke: Palgrave Macmillan

Fontana G, Sawyer M (2016) Towards Post-Keynesian Ecological Macroeconomics. *Ecological Economics* 121: 186–95. http://dx.doi.org/10.1016/j.ecolecon.2015.03.017

Forrester JW (1971) *World Dynamics.* Cambridge, MA: Wright-Allen Press

Forrester JW (1973) *World Dynamics*, 2nd edn. Cambridge, MA: Wright-Allen Press

Forrester JW (1995) The Beginning of System Dynamics. *The McKinsey Quarterly* 1995 (4): 4–17

Forrester JW (2003) Dynamic Models of Economic Systems and Industrial Organizations: Note to the Faculty Research Seminar. From Jay W. Forrester. November 5, 1956. *System Dynamics Review* 19 (4): 329–45

Forrester JW, Gilbert WL, Nathaniel JM (1974) The Debate on 'World Dynamics': A Response to Nordhaus. *Policy Sciences* 5 (2): 169–90

Friedman M (1953) The Methodology of Positive Economics. In: *Essays in Positive Economics.* Chicago, IL: University of Chicago Press, pp 3–43

Friedman M (1969) The Optimum Quantity of Money. In: *The Optimum Quantity of Money and Other Essays.* Chicago: Macmillan, pp 1–50

Friedman M (1983) A Monetarist View. *Journal of Economic Education* 14 (4): 44–55

Friedman M (2007) The Methodology of Positive Economics. In: Hausman D (ed) *The Philosophy of Economics: An Anthology.* Cambridge: Cambridge University Press, pp 145–78

Frisch R (1933) Propagation Problems and Impulse Problems in Dynamic Economics. In: Cassel G (ed) *Economic Essays in Honour of Gustav Cassel.* London: George Allen & Unwin

Fullbrook E (2010) Keen, Roubini and Baker win Revere Award for Economics. Real World Economics Review Blog. https://rwer.wordpress.com/2010/05/13/keen-roubini-and-baker-win-revere-award-for-economics-2/

Fullwiler ST (2003) Timeliness and the Fed's Daily Tactics. *Journal of Economic Issues* 37 (4): 851–80. https://doi.org/10.1080/00213624.2003.11506634

Fullwiler ST (2005) Paying Interest on Reserve Balances: It's More Significant than You Think. *Journal of Economic Issues* 39 (2): 543–50. https://doi.org/10.1080/00213624.2005.11506833

Fullwiler ST (2013) An Endogenous Money Perspective on the Post-Crisis Monetary Policy Debate. *Review of Keynesian Economics* 1 (2): 171–94. https://doi.org/10.4337/roke.2013.02.02

Garegnani P (1970) Heterogeneous Capital, the Production Function and the Theory of Distribution. *Review of Economic Studies* 37 (3): 407–36

Garrett L (1995) *The Coming Plague: Newly Emerging Diseases in a World out of Balance.* New York: Penguin

Garrett TJ (2012a) Modes of Growth in Dynamic Systems. *Proceedings of the Royal Society A: Mathematical, Physical and Engineering Sciences* 468: 2532–49. https://doi.org/10.1098/rspa.2012.0039

Garrett TJ (2012b) No Way Out? The Double-Bind in Seeking Global Prosperity alongside Mitigated Climate Change. *Earth System Dynamics* 3: 1–17. https://doi.org/10.5194/esd-3-1-2012

Garrett TJ (2014) Long-run Evolution of the Global Economy: 1. Physical Basis. *Earth's Future* 2: 127–51. https://doi.org/10.1002/2013EF000171

Garrett TJ, Grasselli M, Keen S (2020) Past World Economic Production Constrains Current Energy Demands: Persistent Scaling with Implications for Economic Growth and Climate Change Mitigation. *PLoS ONE* 15 (8): e0237672. https://doi.org/10.1371/journal.pone.0237672

Garver FB, Seidler G, Reynolds LG, Boddy FM, Tucker RS (1938) Corporate Price Policies. *The American Economic Review* 28 (1): 86–9

Georgescu-Roegen N (1970) The Economics of Production. *The American Economic Review* 60 (2): 1–9

Georgescu-Roegen N (1979) Myths about Energy and Matter. *Growth and Change* 10 (1): 16–23. https://doi.org/10.1111/j.1468-2257.1979.tb00819.x

Georgescu-Roegen N (1986) The Entropy Law and the Economic Process in Retrospect. *Eastern Economic Journal* 12 (1): 3–25

Georgescu-Roegen N (1999) The Economics of Production: Richard T. Ely Lecture. In: Ayres RU, Button K, Nijkamp P (eds) *Global Aspects of the Environment. Volume 1.* Cheltenham: Elgar, pp 287–95

Georgescu-Roegen N (2004) What Thermodynamics and Biology Can Teach Economists. In: Zamagni S, Agliardi E (eds) *Time in Economic Theory.* Cheltenham: Elgar, pp 358–66

Gleeson-White J (2011) *Double Entry.* Sydney: Allen and Unwin

Godley W (1999) Money and Credit in a Keynesian Model of Income Determination. *Cambridge Journal of Economics* 23 (4): 393–411

Godley W (2001) The Developing Recession in the United

States. *Banca Nazionale del Lavoro Quarterly Review* 54 (219): 417–25

Godley W (2004) Money and Credit in a Keynesian Model of Income Determination: Corrigenda. *Cambridge Journal of Economics* 28 (3): 469

Godley W, Izurieta A (2002) The Case for a Severe Recession. *Challenge* 45 (2): 27–51

Godley W, Lavoie M (2007) A Simple Model of Three Economies with Two Currencies: The Eurozone and the USA. *Cambridge Journal of Economics* 31 (1): 1–23

Godley W, Wray LR (2000) Is Goldilocks Doomed? *Journal of Economic Issues* 34 (1): 201–6

Gooding T (2014) Modelling Society's Evolutionary Forces. *Journal of Artificial Societies and Social Simulation* 17 (3): 3. https://doi.org/10.18564/jasss.2497

Gooding T (2019) *Economics for a Fairer Society: Going Back to Basics using Agent-Based Models.* London: Springer International Publishing

Goodwin RM (1966) Cycles and Growth: A Growth Cycle. *Econometrica* 34 (5 Supplement): 46

Goodwin RM (1967) A Growth Cycle. In: Feinstein CH (ed) *Socialism, Capitalism and Economic Growth.* Cambridge: Cambridge University Press, pp 54–8

Goodwin RM (1982) *Essays in Economic Dynamics.* London: Macmillan

Goodwin RM (1986a) The Economy as an Evolutionary Pulsator. *Journal of Economic Behavior and Organization* 7 (4): 341–9

Goodwin RM (1986b) Swinging along the Turnpike with von Neumann and Sraffa. *Cambridge Journal of Economics* 10 (3): 203–10

Goodwin RM, Punzo LF (1987) *The Dynamics of a Capitalist Economy: A Multisectoral Approach.* Boulder, CO: Westview Press

Goodwin RM, Wagener HJ, Drukker JW (1986) The M-K-S System: The Functioning and Evolution of Capitalism. In: *The Economic Law of Motion of Modern Society:*

A Marx-Keynes-Schumpeter Centennial. Cambridge: Cambridge University Press, pp 14–21

Gorman WM (1953) Community Preference Fields. *Econometrica* 21 (1): 63–80

Graeber D (2011) *Debt: The First 5,000 Years*. New York: Melville House

Grasselli M, Costa Lima B (2012) An Analysis of the Keen Model for Credit Expansion, Asset Price Bubbles and Financial Fragility. *Mathematics and Financial Economics* 6: 191–210. https://doi.org/10.1007/s11579-012-0071-8

Grasselli MR, Nguyen-Huu A (2018) Inventory Growth Cycles with Debt-Financed Investment. *Structural Change and Economic Dynamics* 44: 1–13. https://doi.org/10.1016/j.strueco.2018.01.003

Graziani A (1989) The Theory of the Monetary Circuit. Thames Papers in Political Economy TP/PPE/89/1

Greenhill S (2008) 'It's Awful – Why Did Nobody See It Coming?': The Queen Gives her Verdict on Global Credit Crunch. *Mail Online*, 6 November

Hall CAS (2011) Introduction to Special Issue on New Studies in EROI (Energy Return on Investment). *Sustainability* (Basel, Switzerland) 3 (10): 1773–7. https://doi.org/10.3390/su3101773

Hall CAS, Day JW (2009) Revisiting the Limits to Growth After Peak Oil. *American Scientist* 97 (3): 230–7

Hall CAS, Lindenberger D, Kümmel R, Kroeger T, Eichhorn W (2001) The Need to Reintegrate the Natural Sciences with Economics. *BioScience* 51 (8): 663–73

Hall RE (1988) The Relation between Price and Marginal Cost in US Industry. *Journal of Political Economy* 96 (5): 921–47

Hall RL, Hitch CJ (1939) Price Theory and Business Behaviour. *Oxford Economic Papers* (2): 12–45

Hamouda OF, Harcourt GC (1988) Post Keynesianism: From Criticism to Coherence? *Bulletin of Economic Research* 40 (1): 1–33

Harcourt GC (1972) *Some Cambridge Controversies in the*

Theory of Capital. Cambridge: Cambridge University Press

Hicks JR (1935) Wages and Interest: The Dynamic Problem. *The Economic Journal* 45 (179): 456–68

Hicks JR (1937) Mr. Keynes and the 'Classics': A Suggested Interpretation. *Econometrica* 5 (2): 147–59

Hicks JR (1981) IS-LM: An Explanation. *Journal of Post Keynesian Economics* 3 (2): 139–54

Holmes AR (1969) Operational Constraints on the Stabilization of Money Supply Growth. Paper presented at the Controlling Monetary Aggregates conference, Nantucket Island, pp 65–77

Hudson M (2004) The Archaeology of Money: Debt versus Barter Theories of Money's Origins. In: Wray LR (ed) *Credit and State Theories of Money: The Contributions of A. Mitchell Innes.* Cheltenham: Edward Elgar, pp 99–127

Hudson M (2018) ... *and Forgive Them Their Debts: Lending, Foreclosure and Redemption from Bronze Age Finance to the Jubilee Year.* New York: Islet

Ireland PN (2011) A New Keynesian Perspective on the Great Recession. *Journal of Money, Credit, and Banking* 43 (1): 31–54. https://doi.org/10.1111/j.1538-4616.2010.00364.x

Janeway W (2012) *Doing Capitalism in the Innovation Economy.* Cambridge: Cambridge University Press

Jevons WS (1888) *The Theory of Political Economy.* London: Macmillan

Jordà Ò, Schularick M, Taylor AM (2011) Financial Crises, Credit Booms, and External Imbalances: 140 Years of Lessons. *IMF Economic Review* 59 (2): 340–78. https://doi.org/10.1057/imfer.2011.8

Jordà Ò, Knoll K, Kuvshinov D, Schularick M, Taylor AM (2019) The Rate of Return on Everything, 1870–2015. *The Quarterly Journal of Economics* 134 (3): 1225–98. https://doi.org/10.1093/qje/qjz012

Kalecki M (1935) A Macrodynamic Theory of Business Cycles. *Econometrica* 3 (3): 327–44

Kalecki M (1937) A Theory of the Business Cycle. *The Review of Economic Studies* 4 (2): 77–97

Kalecki M (1941) A Theory of Long-Run Distribution of the Product of Industry. *Oxford Economic Papers* (5): 31–41

Kalecki M (1942) Mr. Whitman on the Concept of 'Degree of Monopoly' – A Comment. *The Economic Journal* 52 (205): 121–7

Kalecki M (1949) A New Approach to the Problem of Business Cycles. *The Review of Economic Studies* 16 (2): 57–64

Kalecki M (1962) Observations on the Theory of Growth. *The Economic Journal* 72 (285): 134–53

Kalecki M (1968) Trend and Business Cycles Reconsidered. *The Economic Journal* 78 (310): 263–76

Kalecki M (1971) Class Struggle and the Distribution of National Income. *Kyklos* 24 (1): 1–9. https://doi.org/10.1111/j.1467-6435.1971.tb00148.x

Keen S (1993a) The Misinterpretation of Marx's Theory of Value. *Journal of the History of Economic Thought* 15 (2): 282–300

Keen S (1993b) Use-Value, Exchange Value, and the Demise of Marx's Labor Theory of Value. *Journal of the History of Economic Thought* 15 (1): 107–21

Keen S (1995) Finance and Economic Breakdown: Modeling Minsky's 'Financial Instability Hypothesis'. *Journal of Post Keynesian Economics* 17 (4): 607–35

Keen S (1998) Answers (and Questions) for Sraffians (and Kaleckians). *Review of Political Economy* 10 (1): 73–87

Keen S (2000) The Nonlinear Economics of Debt Deflation. In: Barnett WA, Chiarella C, Keen S, Marks R, Schnabl H (eds) *Commerce, Complexity, and Evolution: Topics in Economics, Finance, Marketing, and Management: Proceedings of the Twelfth International Symposium in Economic Theory and Econometrics*. New York: Cambridge University Press, pp 83–110

Keen S (2006) Steve Keen's Monthly Debt Report

November 2006 'The Recession We Can't Avoid?'. Steve Keen's Debtwatch, vol 1. Sydney

Keen S (2007) Deeper in Debt: Australia's Addiction to Borrowed Money. Occasional Papers. Centre for Policy Development, Sydney

Keen S (2011) *Debunking Economics: The Naked Emperor Dethroned?*, 2nd edn. London: Zed Books

Keen S (2013a) A Monetary Minsky Model of the Great Moderation and the Great Recession. *Journal of Economic Behavior & Organization* 86: 221–35. https://dx.doi.org/10.1016/j.jebo.2011.01.010

Keen S (2013b) Predicting the 'Global Financial Crisis': Post-Keynesian Macroeconomics. *Economic Record* 89 (285): 228–54. https://dx.doi.org/10.1111/1475-4932.12016

Keen S (2015a) Is Neoclassical Economics Mathematical? Is There a Non-Neoclassical Mathematical Economics? In: Morgan J (ed) *What is Neoclassical Economics? Debating the Origins, Meaning and Significance.* Abingdon: Routledge, pp 238–54

Keen S (2015b) Post Keynesian Theories of Crisis. *American Journal of Economics and Sociology* 74 (2): 298–324

Keen S (2020a) The Appallingly Bad Neoclassical Economics of Climate Change. *Globalizations* 1–29. https://dx.doi.org/10.1080/14747731.2020.1807856

Keen S (2020b) Emergent Macroeconomics: Deriving Minsky's Financial Instability Hypothesis Directly from Macroeconomic Definitions. *Review of Political Economy* 32 (3): 342–70. https://dx.doi.org/10.1080/09538259.2020.1810887

Keen S, Ayres RU, Standish R (2019) A Note on the Role of Energy in Production. *Ecological Economics* 157: 40–6. https://doi.org/10.1016/j.ecolecon.2018.11.002

Kelton S (2020) *The Deficit Myth: Modern Monetary Theory and the Birth of the People's Economy.* New York: PublicAffairs

Keynes JM (1936) *The General Theory of Employment, Interest and Money.* London: Macmillan

Keynes JM (1937) The General Theory of Employment. *The Quarterly Journal of Economics* 51 (2): 209–23

Kihlstrom RE, Mas-Colell A, Sonnenschein H (1976) The Demand Theory of the Weak Axiom of Revealed Preference. *Econometrica* 44 (5): 971–8. https://doi.org/10.2307/1911539

King CW (2020) *The Economic Superorganism: Beyond the Competing Narratives on Energy, Growth, and Policy.* New York: Springer

King JE (2003) *A History of Post Keynesian Economics Since 1936.* Aldershot: Edward Elgar

King JE (ed) (2012) *The Elgar Companion to Post Keynesian Economics*, 2nd edn. Aldershot: Edward Elgar

King JE (2014) *The Microfoundations Delusion.* Cheltenham: Edward Elgar

Kirman A (1989) The Intrinsic Limits of Modern Economic Theory: The Emperor Has No Clothes. *Economic Journal* 99 (395): 126–39

Knapp GF (1924) *The State Theory of Money.* London: Macmillan

Komlos J (2021) The Actual US Unemployment Rate in 2019 Was Twice the Official Rate, and the Phillips Curve. *Challenge* 64 (1): 51–74. https://dx.doi.org/10.1080/05775132.2020.1863547

Kriesler P (1988) Kalecki's Pricing Theory Revisited. *Journal of Post Keynesian Economics* 11 (1): 108–30

Krugman P (2009) Liquidity Preference, Loanable Funds, and Niall Ferguson (Wonkish). *New York Times*, 2 May

Krugman P (2011a) Debt Is (Mostly) Money We Owe to Ourselves. *New York Times*, 28 December

Krugman P (2011b) Liquidity Preference and Loanable Funds, Still (Wonkish). *New York Times*, 3 June

Krugman P (2012) *End this Depression Now!* New York: W.W. Norton

Krugman P (2013) Commercial Banks As Creators of 'Money'. *New York Times*, 24 August

Krugman P (2014) A Monetary Puzzle. *New York Times*, 28 April

Krugman P (2015a) Debt Is Money We Owe To Ourselves. *New York Times*, 6 February

Krugman P (2015b) Debt: A Thought Experiment. *New York Times*, 6 February

Kuhn T (1970) *The Structure of Scientific Revolutions*, 2nd edn. Chicago, IL: University of Chicago Press

Kumhof M, Jakab Z (2015) Banks are Not Intermediaries of Loanable Funds – And Why This Matters. Working Paper, Bank of England, London

Kumhof M, Rancière R, Winant P (2015) Inequality, Leverage, and Crises. *The American Economic Review* 105 (3): 1217–45. https://dx.doi.org/10.1257/aer.20110683

Kümmel R (2011) *The Second Law of Economics: Energy, Entropy, and the Origins of Wealth*. New York: Springer

Kümmel R, Ayres RU, Lindenberger D (2010) Thermodynamic Laws, Economic Methods and the Productive Power of Energy. *Journal of Non-Equilibrium Thermodynamics* 35: 145–79

Kümmel R, Lindenberger D, Weiser F (2015) The Economic Power of Energy and the Need to Integrate It with Energy Policy. *Energy Policy* 86: 833–43. https://dx.doi.org/10.1016/j.enpol.2015.07.026

Kypke KL, Langford WF, Willms AR (2020) Anthropocene Climate Bifurcation. *Nonlinear Processes in Geophysics* 27(3): 391–409. https://dx.doi.org/10.5194/npg-27-391-2020

Lavoie M (2015a) *Post-Keynesian Economics: New Foundations*. Cheltenham: Edward Elgar

Lavoie M (2015b) Should Heterodox Economics Be Taught in Economics Departments, Or Is There any Room for Backwater Economics? INET Economics. INET, New York

Lavoie M, Godley W (2001) Kaleckian Models of Growth in a Coherent Stock-Flow Monetary Framework: A Kaldorian View. *Journal of Post Keynesian Economics* 24 (2): 277–311

Lawson T (2013) What is this 'School' Called Neoclassical

Economics? *Cambridge Journal of Economics* 37: 947–83. https://dx.doi.org/10.1093/cje/bet027

Lazear EP, Marron DB (2009) Economic Report of the President. Washington, DC: US Government Printing Office

Lee FS (2018) *Microeconomic Theory: A Heterodox Approach*. London: Routledge

Leijonhufvud A (1973) Life Among the Econ. *Economic Inquiry* 11 (3): 327–37

Lenton TM, Ciscar J-C (2013) Integrating Tipping Points into Climate Impact Assessments. *Climatic Change* 117 (3): 585–97. https://dx.doi.org/10.1007/s10584-012-0572-8

Lenton TM, Held H, Kriegler E, Hall JW, Lucht W, Rahmstorf S, Schellnhuber HJ (2008) Tipping Elements in the Earth's Climate System. *Proceedings of the National Academy of Sciences* 105 (6): 1786–93. https://dx.doi.org/10.1073/pnas.0705414105

Lester RA (1946) Shortcomings of Marginal Analysis for Wage-Employment Problems. *The American Economic Review* 36 (1): 63–82

Li T-Y, Yorke JA (1975) Period Three Implies Chaos. *The American Mathematical Monthly* 82 (10): 985–92

Lomborg B (2020) Welfare in the 21st Century: Increasing Development, Reducing Inequality, the Impact of Climate Change, and the Cost of Climate Policies. *Technological Forecasting and Social Change* 156: 119981. https://doi.org/10.1016/j.techfore.2020.119981

Lorenz EN (1963) Deterministic Nonperiodic Flow. *Journal of the Atmospheric Sciences* 20 (2): 130–41. https://dx.doi.org/10.1175/1520-0469(1963)020<0130:DNF>2.0.CO;2

Lotka AJ (1920) Analytical Note on Certain Rhythmic Relations in Organic Systems. *Proceedings of the National Academy of Sciences of the United States of America* 6 (7): 410–15. https://dx.doi.org/10.1073/pnas.6.7.410

Lucas RE, Jr. (2003) Macroeconomic Priorities. *The*

American Economic Review 93 (1): 1–14. https://dx.doi.org/10.1257/000282803321455133

Lucas RE, Jr. (2004) Keynote Address to the 2003 HOPE Conference: My Keynesian Education. *History of Political Economy* 36: 12–24. https://doi.org/10.1215/00182702-36-Suppl_1-12

Maddison D, Rehdanz K (2011) The Impact of Climate on Life Satisfaction. *Ecological Economics* 70 (12): 2437–45. https://doi.org/10.1016/j.ecolecon.2011.07.027

Major I, King RF, Marian CG (2016) Anticommons, the Coase Theorem and the Problem of Bundling Inefficiency. *International Journal of the Commons* 10 (1): 244–64

Malthus TR (1798) *An essay on the principle of population, as it affects the future improvement of society: with remarks on the speculations of Mr. Godwin, M. Condorcet and other writers*. London: J. Johnson

Mandelbrot BB, Hudson RL (2004) *The (Mis)Behaviour of Markets: A Fractal View of Risk, Ruin and Reward*. London: Profile

Mankiw NG (2001) *Principles of Microeconomics*, 2nd edn. Stamford, CT: South-Western College Publishers

Mankiw NG (2012) *Principles of Macroeconomics*, 6th edn. Mason, OH: South-Western, Cengage Learning

Mankiw NG (2016) *Macroeconomics*, 9th edn. New York: Macmillan

Mankiw NG, Phelps ES, Romer PM (1995) The Growth of Nations. *Brookings Papers on Economic Activity* 1995: 1: 275–326

Marglin SA, Schor JB (1992) *Golden Age of Capitalism*. Oxford: Clarendon Press

Marx K (1857 [1993]) *Grundrisse: Foundations of the Critique of Political Economy*. London: Penguin Classics

Marx K (1867) *Capital*. Moscow: Progress Press

Marx K (1894) *Capital, Volume III*. Moscow: International Publishers

Marx K, Engels F (1848 [2017]) *The Communist Manifesto*. London: Pluto Press

Mas-Colell A, Whinston MD, Green JR (1995) *Microeconomic Theory*. New York: Oxford University Press

Mazzucato M (2015) *The Entrepreneurial State: Debunking Public vs. Private Sector Myths*. New York: Anthem Press

Mazzucato M (2019) *The Value of Everything: Making and Taking in the Global Economy*. London: Penguin Books

McCombie JSL (1998) 'Are There Laws of Production?': An Assessment of the Early Criticisms of the Cobb-Douglas Production Function. *Review of Political Economy* 10 (2): 141–73. https://dx.doi.org/10.1080/09538259800000023

McCombie JSL (2000) The Solow Residual, Technical Change, and Aggregate Production Functions. *Journal of Post Keynesian Economics* 23 (2): 267–97. https://doi.org/10.1080/01603477.2000.11490280

McLeay M, Radia A, Thomas R (2014a) Money Creation in the Modern Economy. *Bank of England Quarterly Bulletin* 2014 Q1: 14–27

McLeay M, Radia A, Thomas R (2014b) Money in the Modern Economy: An Introduction. *Bank of England Quarterly Bulletin* 2014 Q1: 4–13

Meadows DH (2008) *Thinking in Systems: A Primer*. Hartford, VT: Chelsea Green Publishing

Meadows DH, Randers J, Meadows D (1972) *The Limits to Growth*. New York: Signet

Means GC (1935) Price Inflexibility and the Requirements of a Stabilizing Monetary Policy. *Journal of the American Statistical Association* 30 (190): 401–13

Means GC (1936) Notes on Inflexible Prices. *The American Economic Review* 26 (1): 23–35

Means GC (1972) The Administered-Price Thesis Reconfirmed. *The American Economic Review* 62 (3): 292–306

Mendelsohn R, Schlesinger M, Williams L (2000) Comparing Impacts across Climate Models. *Integrated*

Assessment 1 (1): 37–48. https://dx.doi.org/10.1023/a:1019111327619

Minsky HP (1963) Can 'It' Happen Again? In: Carson D (ed) *Banking and Monetary Studies*. Homewood, IL: Richard D Irwin, pp 101–11

Minsky HP (1972) Financial Instability Revisited: The Economics of Disaster. In: Board of Governors of the Federal Reserve System (ed) *Reappraisal of the Federal Reserve Discount Mechanism*. Washington, DC: Board of Governors of the Federal Reserve System, pp 95–136

Minsky HP (1975) *John Maynard Keynes. Columbia Essays on the Great Economists*. New York: Columbia University Press

Minsky HP (1977) The Financial Instability Hypothesis: An Interpretation of Keynes and an Alternative to 'Standard' Theory. *Nebraska Journal of Economics and Business* 16 (1): 5–16

Minsky HP (1978) The Financial Instability Hypothesis: A Restatement. Thames Papers in Political Economy

Minsky HP (1982) *Can 'It' Happen Again?: Essays on Instability and Finance*. Armonk, NY: M.E. Sharpe

Minsky HP (1990) Longer Waves in Financial Relations: Financial Factors in the More Severe Depressions. In: Mayer T (ed) *Monetary Theory*. Aldershot: Elgar, pp 352–63

Minsky HP, Vaughan MD (1990) Debt and Business Cycles. *Business Economics* 25 (3): 23–8

Mitchell M (2009) *Complexity: A Guided Tour*. Oxford: Oxford University Press

Mitchell WF (1987) The Nairu, Structural Imbalance and the Macroequilibrium Unemployment Rate. *Australian Economic Papers* 26 (48): 101–18. https://doi.org/10.1111/j.1467-8454.1987.tb00450.x

Mitchell WF (1994) Restoring Full Employment: A Problem of Policy Balance. *Australian Economic Review* 27 (1): 24–30. https://doi.org/10.1111/j.1467-8462.1994.tb00822.x

Mitchell WF, Mosler WB (2002) Fiscal Policy and the Job

Guarantee. *Australian Journal of Labour Economics* 5 (2): 243–59

Mitchell WF, Watts M (2002) Restoring Full Employment: The Job Guarantee. In: Carlson E, Mitchell W (eds) *The Urgency of Full Employment.* Sydney: Centre for Applied Economic Research, pp 95–114

Mitchell WF, Wray LR, Watts M (2019) *Macroeconomics.* London: Red Globe Press

Modigliani F, Merton HM (1958) The Cost of Capital, Corporation Finance and the Theory of Investment. *The American Economic Review* 48 (3): 261–97

Moore BJ (1979) The Endogenous Money Stock. *Journal of Post Keynesian Economics* 2 (1): 49–70. https://doi.org/10.1080/01603477.1979.11489137

Moore BJ (1988) *Horizontalists and Verticalists: The Macroeconomics of Credit Money.* Cambridge: Cambridge University Press

Moore BJ (1997) Reconciliation of the Supply and Demand for Endogenous Money. *Journal of Post Keynesian Economics* 19 (3): 423–8. https://doi.org/10.1080/0160 3477.1997.11490119

Moore BJ (2001) Some Reflections on Endogenous Money. In: Rochon L-P, Vernengo M (eds) *Credit, Interest Rates and the Open Economy: Essays on Horizontalism.* Cheltenham: Edward Elgar, pp 11–30

Mora C, Dousset B, Caldwell IR, Powell FE, Geronimo RC, Bielecki CR, Counsell CWW, Dietrich BS, Johnston ET, Louis LV, Lucas MP, McKenzie MM, Shea AG, Tseng H, Giambelluca TW, Leon LR, Hawkins E, Trauernicht C (2017) Global Risk of Deadly Heat. *Nature Climate Change* 7 (7). doi:10.1038/nclimate3322

Mosler W (1998) Full Employment and Price Stability. *Journal of Post Keynesian Economics* 20 (2): 167–82

Mosler W (2010) *The Seven Deadly Innocent Frauds of Economic Policy.* St. Croix, USVI: Valance Co

Murphy T (2012) Exponential Economist Meets Finite Physicist. Do the Math. San Diego

Musgrave A (1981) 'Unreal Assumptions' in Economic

Theory: The F-Twist Untwisted. *Kyklos* 34 (3): 377–87. https://doi.org/10.1111/j.1467-6435.1981.tb01195.x

Musk E (2017) Making Humans a Multi-Planetary Species. *New Space* 5 (2): 46–61. https://doi.org/10.1089/space.2017.29009.emu

Muth JF (1961) Rational Expectations and the Theory of Price Movements. *Econometrica* 29 (3): 315–35

National Research Council (1978) *International Perspectives on the Study of Climate and Society: Report of the International Workshop on Climate Issues*. Washington, DC: The National Academies Press

Nitzan J, Bichler S (2009) *Capital as Power: A Study of Order and Creorder*. London: Routledge

Nordhaus WD (1973) World Dynamics: Measurement without Data. *The Economic Journal* 83 (332): 1156–83. https://doi.org/10.2307/2230846

Nordhaus WD (1974a) The 1974 Report of the President's Council of Economic Advisers: Energy in the Economic Report. *The American Economic Review* 64 (4): 558–65

Nordhaus WD (1974b) Resources as a Constraint on Growth. *The American Economic Review* 64 (2): 22–6

Nordhaus WD (1976) Strategies for the Control of Carbon Dioxide. Cowles Foundation Discussion Paper

Nordhaus WD (1977) Economic Growth and Climate: The Carbon Dioxide Problem. *The American Economic Review* 67 (1): 341–6

Nordhaus WD (1980a) The Energy Crisis and Macroeconomic Policy. *The Energy Journal* 1 (1): 11–19

Nordhaus WD (1980b) Thinking about Carbon Dioxide: Theoretical and Empirical Aspects of Optimal Control Strategies. Cowles Foundation Discussion Paper

Nordhaus WD (1982) How Fast Should We Graze the Global Commons? *The American Economic Review* 72 (2): 242–6

Nordhaus WD (1986) Resources, Technology, and Development: Will the Table Be Bare When Poor

Countries Get There? *Indian Economic Review* 21 (2): 81–94

Nordhaus WD (1991a) The Cost of Slowing Climate Change: A Survey. *The Energy Journal* 12 (1): 37–65

Nordhaus WD (1991b) A Sketch of the Economics of the Greenhouse Effect. *The American Economic Review* 81 (2): 146–50

Nordhaus WD (1991c) To Slow or Not to Slow: The Economics of the Greenhouse Effect. *The Economic Journal* 101 (407): 920–37. doi:10.2307/2233864

Nordhaus WD (1994) Expert Opinion on Climate Change. *American Scientist* 82 (1): 45–51

Nordhaus WD (2013) *The Climate Casino: Risk, Uncertainty, and Economics for a Warming World.* New Haven, CT: Yale University Press

Nordhaus WD (2018a) Nobel Lecture in Economic Sciences. Climate Change: The Ultimate Challenge for Economics. Nobel Prize in Economics Committee. https://www. nobelprize.org/uploads/2018/10/nordhaus-slides.pdf

Nordhaus WD (2018b) Projections and Uncertainties about Climate Change in an Era of Minimal Climate Policies. *American Economic Journal: Economic Policy* 10 (3): 333–60. https://doi.org/10.1257/pol.20170046

Nordhaus WD, Sztorc P (2013) DICE 2013R: Introduction and User's Manual

Nordhaus WD, Houthakker H, Solow R (1973) The Allocation of Energy Resources. *Brookings Papers on Economic Activity* 1973 (3): 529–76. https://doi. org/10.2307/2534202

Orléan A (2015) Economists Also Need Competition. *Le Monde*, 19 January

Oswald A, Stern N (2019) Why Are Economists Letting Down the World on Climate Change? Centre for Economic Policy Research. https://voxeu.org/article/ why-are-economists-letting-down-world-climate-change

Pasinetti LL (1969) Switches of Technique and the 'Rate of Return' in Capital Theory. *The Economic Journal* 79 (315): 508–31. https://doi.org/10.2307/2230379

Peters E (1994) *Fractal Market Analysis: Applying Chaos Theory to Investment and Economics*. New York: Wiley

Peters E (1996) *Chaos and Order in the Capital Markets: A New View of Cycles, Prices, and Market Volatility*. New York: Wiley

Peters E (2003) Simple and Complex Market Inefficiencies: Integrating Efficient Markets, Behavioral Finance, and Complexity. *Journal of Behavioral Finance* 4 (4): 225–33

Peters O (2019) The Ergodicity Problem in Economics. *Nature Physics* 15 (12): 1216–21. https://doi.org/10.1038/s41567-019-0732-0

Peters O, Gell-Mann M (2016) Evaluating Gambles Using Dynamics. *Chaos: An Interdisciplinary Journal of Nonlinear Science* 26 (2): 023103. https://doi.org/10.1063/1.4940236

Phillips AW (1950) Mechanical Models in Economic Dynamics. *Economica* 17 (67): 283–305

Phillips AW (1954) Stabilisation Policy in a Closed Economy. *The Economic Journal* 64 (254): 290–323

Phillips AW (1956) Some Notes on the Estimation of Time-Forms of Reactions in Interdependent Dynamic Systems. *Economica* 23 (90): 99–113

Phillips AW (1957) Stabilisation Policy and the Time-Forms of Lagged Responses. *The Economic Journal* 67 (266): 265–77

Phillips AW (1958) The Relation between Unemployment and the Rate of Change of Money Wage Rates in the United Kingdom, 1861–1957. *Economica* 25 (100): 283–99

Phillips AW (1959) The Estimation of Parameters in Systems of Stochastic Differential Equations. *Biometrika* 46 (1/2): 67–76

Phillips AW (1968) Models for the Control of Economic Fluctuations. In: *Scientific Growth Systems, Mathematical Model Building in Economics and Industry*. London: Griffin, pp 159–65

Pigou AC (1927) *Industrial Fluctuations*. London: Macmillan

Planck M (1949) *Scientific Autobiography and Other Papers*. London: Williams & Norgate

Pomeau Y, Manneville P (1980) Intermittent Transition to Turbulence in Dissipative Dynamical Systems. *Communications in Mathematical Physics* 74: 189–97

Quiggin J (2010) *Zombie Economics: How Dead Ideas Still Walk Among Us*. Princeton, NJ: Princeton University Press

Radzicki MJ (2003) Mr. Hamilton, Mr. Forrester, and a Foundation for Evolutionary Economics. *Journal of Economic Issues* 37 (1): 133–73. https://doi.org/10.108 0/00213624.2003.11506561

Radzicki MJ, Tauheed L (2009) In Defense of System Dynamics: A Response to Professor Hayden. *Journal of Economic Issues* 43 (4): 1043–61. https://doi.org/ 10.2753/JEI0021-3624430411

Ramsey FP (1928) A Mathematical Theory of Saving. *The Economic Journal* 38 (152): 543–59. https://doi. org/10.2307/2224098

Raworth K (2017) *Doughnut Economics: Seven Ways to Think Like a 21st-Century Economist*. White River Junction, VT: Chelsea Green Publishing

Rehdanz K, Maddison D (2005) Climate and Happiness. *Ecological Economics* 52 (1): 111–25. https://doi. org/10.1016/j.ecolecon.2004.06.015

Ricardo D (1817) *On the Principles of Political Economy and Taxation*. London: John Murray

Roberts A (2012) *America's First Great Depression: Economic Crisis and Political Disorder after the Panic of 1837*. Ithaca, NY: Cornell University Press

Robinson J (1964) Pre-Keynesian Theory After Keynes. *Australian Economic Papers* 3 (1–2): 25–35. https://doi. org/10.1111/j.1467-8454.1964.tb00729.x

Robinson J (1971a) The Existence of Aggregate Production Functions: Comment. *Econometrica* 39 (2): 405. https://doi.org/0012-9682(197103)39:2<405:TEOAPF >2.0.CO;2-P

Robinson J (1971b) The Measure of Capital: The End of the Controversy. *Economic Journal* 81 (323): 597–602. https://doi.org/10.2307/2229853

Romer P (2016) The Trouble with Macroeconomics. https://paulromer.net/trouble-with-macroeconomics-update/WP-Trouble.pdf

Samuelson PA (1956) Social Indifference Curves. *The Quarterly Journal of Economics* 70 (1): 1–22

Samuelson PA (1966) A Summing Up. *The Quarterly Journal of Economics* 80 (4): 568–83

Samuelson PA, Nordhaus WD (2010a) *Economics*, 19th edn. New York: McGraw-Hill

Samuelson PA, Nordhaus WD (2010b) *Microeconomics*, 19th edn. New York: McGraw-Hill Irwin

Sargent TJ, Stachurski J (2020a) *Advanced Quantitative Economics with Python*, https://python-advanced.quantecon.org/

Sargent TJ, Stachurski J (2020b) *Quantitative Economics with Python*, https://python.quantecon.org/intro.html

Sargent TJ, Wallace N (1976) Rational Expectations and the Theory of Economic Policy. *Journal of Monetary Economics* 2 (2): 169–83. https://doi.org/10.1016/0304-3932(76)90032-5

Say JB (1821) Letters to Mr. Malthus on several subjects of political economy and on the cause of the stagnation of commerce: to which is added, A catechism of political economy, or, Familiar conversations on the manner in which wealth is produced, distributed, and consumed in society (trans J Richter). London: Printed for Sherwood, Neely, and Jones

Schularick M, Taylor AM (2012) Credit Booms Gone Bust: Monetary Policy, Leverage Cycles, and Financial Crises, 1870–2008. *The American Economic Review* 102 (2): 1029–61

Schumpeter JA (1928) The Instability of Capitalism. *The Economic Journal* 38 (151): 361–86

Schumpeter JA (1934) *The Theory of Economic Development: An Inquiry into Profits, Capital, Credit,*

Interest and the Business Cycle. Cambridge, MA: Harvard University Press

Shafer W, Sonnenschein H (1982) Market Demand and Excess Demand Functions. In: Arrow KJ, Intriligator MD (eds) *Handbook of Mathematical Economics, vol 2.* Amsterdam: North-Holland, pp 671–93

Shaikh A (1974) Laws of Production and Laws of Algebra: The Humbug Production Function. *Review of Economics and Statistics* 56 (1): 115–20. https://doi.org/10.2307/1927538

Shaikh A (2005) Nonlinear Dynamics and Pseudo-Production Functions. *Eastern Economic Journal* 31 (3): 447–66

Sippel R (1997) An Experiment on the Pure Theory of Consumer's Behaviour. *The Economic Journal* 107 (444): 1431–44

Smil V (1987) A Perspective on Global Environmental Crises. *Futures* 19 (3): 240–53. http://dx.doi.org/10.1016/0016-3287(87)90018-8

Smil V (2017) *Energy and Civilization: A History.* Cambridge, MA: The MIT Press

Smith A (1776) *An Inquiry Into the Nature and Causes of the Wealth of Nations*, vol 2. Glasgow Edition of the Works and Correspondence of Adam Smith. Indianapolis, IN: Liberty Fund

Smith C (1998) *The Science of Energy: A Cultural History of Energy Physics in Victorian Britain.* London: Athlone

Solow RM (2010) Building a Science of Economics for the Real World. House Committee on Science and Technology Subcommittee on Investigations and Oversight, Washington

Sonnenschein H (1972) Market Excess Demand Functions. *Econometrica* 40 (3): 549–63

Sonnenschein H (1973a) The Utility Hypothesis and Market Demand Theory. *Economic Inquiry* 11 (4): 404–10

Sonnenschein H (1973b) Do Walras' Identity and Continuity Characterize the Class of Community Excess Demand

Functions? *Journal of Economic Theory* 6 (4): 345–54. https://doi.org/10.1016/0022-0531(73)90066-5

Sraffa P (1926) The Laws of Returns under Competitive Conditions. *The Economic Journal* 36 (144): 535–50

Sraffa P (1960) *Production of Commodities by Means of Commodities: Prelude to a Critique of Economic Theory*. Cambridge: Cambridge University Press

Sraffa P (1962) Production of Commodities: A Comment. *The Economic Journal* 72 (286): 477–9

Steedman I (1977) *Marx after Sraffa*. London: NLB

Steedman I (1992) Questions for Kaleckians. *Review of Political Economy* 4 (2): 125–51. https://doi.org/10.1080/09538259200000011

Steedman I (1993) Points for Kaleckians. *Review of Political Economy* 5 (1): 113–16. https://doi.org/10.1080/09538259300000006

Steffen W, Rockström J, Richardson K, Lenton TM, Folke C, Liverman D, Summerhayes CP, Barnosky AD, Cornell SE, Crucifix M, Donges JF, Fetzer I, Lade SJ, Scheffer M, Winkelmann R, Schellnhuber HJ (2018) Trajectories of the Earth System in the Anthropocene. *Proceedings of the National Academy of Sciences* 115 (33): 8252–9. https://doi.org/10.1073/pnas.1810141115

Stiglitz JE (1974a) Growth with Exhaustible Natural Resources: Efficient and Optimal Growth Paths. *The Review of Economic Studies* 41 (5): 123–37. https://doi.org/10.2307/2296377

Stiglitz JE (1974b) Growth with Exhaustible Natural Resources: The Competitive Economy. *The Review of Economic Studies* 41 (5): 139–52. https://doi.org/10.2307/2296378

Stiglitz JE (2011) Rethinking Macroeconomics: What Failed, and How to Repair It. *Journal of the European Economic Association* 9 (4): 591–645. https://doi.org/10.1111/j.1542-4774.2011.01030.x

Stiglitz JE (2018) Where Modern Macroeconomics Went Wrong. *Oxford Review of Economic Policy* 34 (1–2): 70–106. https://doi.org/10.1093/oxrep/grx057

Summers L (2013) Larry Summers at IMF Economic Forum, 8 November

Taleb NN (2010) *The Black Swan: The Impact of the Highly Improbable*, rev. edn. London: Penguin

Tol RSJ (2002) Estimates of the Damage Costs of Climate Change. Part 1: Benchmark Estimates. *Environmental and Resource Economics* 21 (1): 47–73. https://doi.org/10.1023/a:1014500930521

Tol RSJ (2009) The Economic Effects of Climate Change. *The Journal of Economic Perspectives* 23 (2): 29–51

Tucker RS (1937) Is There a Tendency for Profits to Equalize? *The American Economic Review* 27 (3): 519–24

Tucker RS (1938) The Reasons for Price Rigidity. *The American Economic Review* 28 (1): 41–54

Turgot M (1774) *Reflections on the Formation and Distribution of Wealth*. London: Spragg

Turner GM (2008) A Comparison of *The Limits to Growth* with 30 Years of Reality. *Global Environmental Change* 18 (3): 397–411. doi:10.1016/j.gloenvcha.2008.05.001

Turner GM (2014) Is Global Collapse Imminent? An Updated Comparison of *The Limits to Growth* with Historical Data. Melbourne Sustainable Society Institute, Melbourne

Vague R (2019) *A Brief History of Doom: Two Hundred Years of Financial Crises*. Philadelphia, PA: University of Pennsylvania Press

Veblen T (1898) Why is Economics not an Evolutionary Science? *The Quarterly Journal of Economics* 12 (4): 373–97

Veblen T (1908) Professor Clark's Economics. *The Quarterly Journal of Economics* 22 (2): 147–95

Veblen T (1909) The Limitations of Marginal Utility. *The Journal of Political Economy* 17 (9): 620–36

Voudouris V, Ayres R, Serrenho A, Kiose D (2015) The Economic Growth Enigma Revisited: The EU-15 Since the 1970s. *Energy Policy* 86: 812–32. https://doi.org/10.1016/j.enpol.2015.04.027

Warren R, Price J, Graham E, Forstenhaeusler N,

VanDerWal J (2018) The Projected Effect on Insects, Vertebrates, and Plants of Limiting Global Warming to 1.5°C rather than 2°C. *Science* 360 (6390): 791–5. https://doi.org/10.1126/science.aar3646

Werner RA (2014a) Can Banks Individually Create Money out of Nothing? The Theories and the Empirical Evidence. *International Review of Financial Analysis* 36: 1–19. https://doi.org/10.1016/j.irfa.2014.07.015

Werner RA (2014b) How Do Banks Create Money, and Why Can Other Firms Not Do The Same? An Explanation for the Coexistence of Lending and Deposit-Taking. *International Review of Financial Analysis* 36: 71–7. http://dx.doi.org/10.1016/j.irfa.2014.10.013

Wheat ID (2007) The Feedback Method. A System Dynamics Approach to Teaching Macroeconomics. The University of Bergen. https://bora.uib.no/handle/1956/2239

Wheat ID (2017) Teaching Endogenous Money with Systems Thinking and Simulation Tools. *International Journal of Pluralism and Economics Education* 8 (3): 219–43. https://doi.org/10.1504/IJPEE.2017.088767

Wigglesworth R (2020) The Debt Bubble Legacy of Economists Modigliani and Miller. *Financial Times*, 18 October

Woit P (2006) *Not Even Wrong: The Failure of String Theory and the Search for Unity in Physical Law*. New York: Basic Books

Wray LR (1994) Government Deficits, Liquidity Preference, and Schumpeterian Innovation. *Economies et Sociétés* 28 (1–2): 39–59

Wray LR (1997) Government as Employer of Last Resort: Full Employment without Inflation. Levy Economics Institute, Working Paper No. 213. http://www.levyinstitute.org/pubs/wp213.pdf

Wray LR (1998) *Understanding Modern Money: The Key to Full Employment and Price Stability*. Cheltenham: Elgar

Zhang L, Bezemer D (2014) From Boom to Bust in the Credit Cycle: The Role of Mortgage Credit. IDEAS Working Paper Series

Index

Planck, Max 5–6, 10
pollution 107, 111
Ponzi schemes 72
Post Keynesian economics 4,
11, 14, 23–4, 26, 50, 54,
102, 108–9, 151–3
Post-Crash Economics
movement 16
post-Neoclassical economic
paradigm
essential elements of 142
mathematical foundation of
143–4
predator-prey model 76–7,
76, 78, 147
pricing 107, 149
'degree of monopoly'
mark-up 128
private debt 4, 5
aggregate demand and
rising 23, 87
and credit 57–8, 58
depressing of economic
activity 65
falling of after Second
World War 64
and Financial Instability
Hypothesis 23
and Great Depression 23
ignoring of by Neoclassical
economists 5, 20, 21, 23,
56, 59, 65
and Minsky's theory of
systemic instability 83–5
Modern Debt Jubilee and
reducing of 66
need to reduce 59, 65
as primary cause of
economic crises 4, 65,
83
rising of and declining

cycles in employment and
inflation 91, 92
rising of in Roaring
Twenties 60, 63
private debt-to-GDP ratio 58,
61–2, 63, 64, 74
dangers of high and need
for reducing 65–6, 74
rise in 60, 61–2, 64–5
production
and Cobb-Douglas
Production Function 102,
105–7
and energy 102–9
and entropy 109
Leontief production
function 102, 105, 106,
107
Marx on 140
and nature 102
Neoclassical model of 127
as output of labour and
capital 102
Physiocratic approach 102
produces a deficit rather
than a surplus 108–9
'Protest Against Autistic
Economics' 16

Quantitative Easing
and Federal Reserve 1, 67–8
and increase in inequality
66–8
*Quarterly Journal of
Economics* 136
Quiggin, John 134

Ramsey, E.P. 141
Randers, J. 147
rational expectations model
124–5